"This book offers a refreshingly honest and thorough exploration into a generational crisis infused with divine opportunity. Christie Penner Worden helps us rediscover Jesus in the midst of chaotic times, turning up the volume on the good news. Read this book and learn to love a generation into their truest identity in Christ. This will help us all become who we were meant to be together!"

DANIELLE STRICKLAND, author, advocate, and communicator

"A Jesus-centered, love-filled, intergenerationally informed engagement with this crucial current question: How shall Christian parents engage their children's wrestling with issues of identity? Highly recommended."

DAVID P. GUSHEE, Distinguished University Professor of Christian Ethics at Mercer University, chair of Christian Social Ethics at Vrije Universiteit (Free University) Amsterdam, senior research fellow at International Baptist Theological Study Centre, and author of *After Evangelicalism: The Path to a New Christianity*

"Christie Penner Worden invites us to think first about how we want to discuss identity before jumping into the who, what, why, and when. She boldly, yet gently, reminds us that at the core of all our theological distinctives lies the centrality of Jesus and his love for all his children. A must-read for parents, grandparents, and ministry leaders who are looking to navigate conversations around identity while truly loving the kids and youth in their care."

NATALIE FRISK, director of curriculum for RaiseUp Faith and author of *Raising Disciples: How to Make Faith Matter for Our Kids*

"In *The Me I Was Made to Be*, Christie Penner Worden invites us into kids' wonderings about identity and points out ways that adults miss the mark in accompanying them. In helping readers grapple with unraveling the complexity of identity, Penner Worden helps readers reconfigure their understanding of Jesus for everybody, child and adult alike."

CHRISTINE J. HONG, associate professor of educational ministry and director of the Doctor of Educational Ministry program at Columbia Theological Seminary

"Christie Penner Worden has written a book that every parent, teacher, leader, and pastor should read. It's colorful, charming, and filled with the deep wisdom we need for this moment. *The Me I Was Mede to Be* will help you navigate difficult conversations with grace, it will empower you to share the love of Jesus with kids, it will give tools to be a non-anxious, Jesus-like presence in people's lives, and maybe most surprising of all, it will remind you of God's deep abiding love for you."

JONNY MORRISON, church planter, pastor, and author of *Prodigal Gospel: Getting Lost and Found Again in the Good News*

THE ME I WAS MADE TO BE

the ME I WAS MADE TO BE

HELPING CHRISTIAN PARENTS
NAVIGATE THE IDENTITY CONVERSATION

CHRISTIE PENNER WORDEN

HERALD PRESS

Harrisonburg, Virginia

Herald Press
PO Box 866, Harrisonburg, Virginia 22803
www.HeraldPress.com

Library of Congress Cataloging-in-Publication Data
Names: Penner Worden, Christie, author.
Title: The me I was made to be : helping Christian parents navigate the
    identity conversation / Christie Penner Worden.
Description: Harrisonburg, Virginia : Herald Press, [2024] | Includes
    bibliographical references.
Identifiers: LCCN 2024016175 (print) | LCCN 2024016176 (ebook) | ISBN
    9781513814841 (paperback) | ISBN 9781513814858 (hardcover) | ISBN
    9781513814865 (ebook)
Subjects: LCSH: Parenting--Religious aspects--Christianity. | Parent and
    teenager--Religious aspects--Christianity. | Identity (Psychology) in
    adolescence. | Identity (Psychology)--Religious aspects--Christianity. |
    Christian teenagers--Religious life. | BISAC: RELIGION / Christian
    Living / Family & Relationships | SELF-HELP / Personal Growth / General
Classification: LCC BV4529 .P428 2024 (print) | LCC BV4529 (ebook) | DDC
    248.8/45--dc23/eng/20240516
LC record available at https://lccn.loc.gov/2024016175
LC ebook record available at https://lccn.loc.gov/2024016176

Study guides are available for many Herald Press titles at www.HeraldPress.com.

THE ME I WAS MADE TO BE
© 2024 by Herald Press, Harrisonburg, Virginia 22803. 800-245-7894. All rights reserved.
Library of Congress Control Number: 2024016175
International Standard Book Number: 978-1-5138-1484-1 (paperback);
    978-1-5138-1485-8 (hardcover); 978-1-5138-1486-5 (ebooks)
Printed in United States of America

28 27 26 25 24   10 9 8 7 6 5 4 3 2 1

To *Ruby, Benaiah, and Elliotte:*

I earned my PhD in life around our kitchen table. You have been the best teachers, and I love you like crazy. Thank you for letting me be the me I was made to be as I learned to allow you to do the same. Live wildly, outrageously magnificent lives because you were made for greatness, bearing the fingerprints of a very great God, love incarnate in Jesus, embodied in each of you by the Holy Spirit.

So do not be afraid of them, for there is nothing concealed that will not be disclosed, or hidden that will not be made known. What I tell you in the dark, speak in the daylight; what is whispered in your ear, proclaim from the roofs. Do not be afraid of those who kill the body but cannot kill the soul. Rather, be afraid of the One who can destroy both soul and body in hell. Are not two sparrows sold for a penny? Yet not one of them will fall to the ground outside your Father's care. And even the very hairs of your head are all numbered. So don't be afraid; you are worth more than many sparrows.
—Matthew 10:26–31

Identity isn't a problem to be solved.
It is a wonder to behold.

CONTENTS

FOREWORD

Christie Penner Worden and I met—as so many do in the 2020s—on the internet, and that connection quickly turned into a video call for one simple reason: we geek out about young people and faith. For my part, I'd been writing to parents about research I'd been involved in on how faith grows in kids and families. Connecting with Christie about her work as a pastor and kids ministry expert was like making an instant bond with someone who does the same weird work you do.

You may or may not know that being a pastor is a weird job, but it's true. On the one hand, we love to consider important questions that influence deep parts of a person's life. On the other hand, if a pastor serves young people—like Christie and I do—you often create a space for others to explore those questions that includes a ridiculous game and a (hopefully) helpful object lesson (like a mango).

Research has long told us that some of the more important questions that young people are asking are about their identity. They don't just wonder, "Who am I?" They wonder whether they are really enough, and can they live in this world feeling at home in their body, and will the adults who are meant to care for them understand if they share more?

A few years ago I was at a roundtable, comprised mainly of adults, where a high school junior shared honestly about the conversations that happened in the cafeteria, in the halls, on their phones. She contrasted those topics with the ones that tended to come up at church, and she closed by saying, "It's not like the stuff at church isn't *interesting*, it's just not helpful for anything my friends are struggling with."

What a heartbreaking, honest thing to say. Because what does Jesus hope for this young person's friends more than to help, in the ways they most need?

You are here because you are an adult who wants to love the kids in your life well. You want to *help* them with this question, in Jesus' name. You may not understand, either, but you're committed to trying. It doesn't matter whether the kids are your own children, extended family, or in your neighborhood or faith community.

That's why I'm so grateful and excited for you to read this book. You'll find that it's not just considering this important question that's top of mind for young people; it's offering possible answers from an expert practitioner and pastor—someone who geeks out entirely on helping young people know Jesus, someone full of love for the young people we get to walk with. Yet, although Christie brings so much expertise to the party, her trust in God's Spirit to work in and speak to *you* will leave you the best kinds of answers—the ones you've intentionally, prayerfully, and thoughtfully discerned for yourself.

I hope you enjoy the journey of this book as much as Christie enjoys mango.

—Meredith Anne Miller
Pastor and author of *Woven: Nurturing a*
Faith Your Kid Doesn't Have to Heal From

INTRODUCTION

Let's have a conversation about identity.

The very definition of the word *conversation* includes the idea of an exchange. I think it will be helpful to keep *exchange* in mind as we navigate a challenging subject. But let me say that I'm sad I cannot actually sit and exchange with each of you; I'd much rather sit at a table, coffee in hand, and talk. We would ask big questions and share ideas, thoughts, and feelings about those questions. And we would pray that God would fill in the gaps between all the unknowns.

This book is meant to facilitate your ability to do just that with *your* people: friends, your kids' friends' parents, your small group at church maybe, your partner. My hope is to set you up with enough hope and enough tenacity so you can lean into the conversation, create safe space for one another, and exchange thoughts, feelings, and questions with those with whom you do life.

But I think you may want or need to have this conversation with other people, too: kids. Whether they're your own kids or kids you love and serve in one way or another, you need to be equipped for this conversation. Not because I think it's necessarily your job to tackle it, but rather because kids are already having it. And a conversation with them needs to be an exchange, too.

This conversation is different for kids today than it likely was for us when we were growing up. Kids today don't know that things weren't always the way they are now, and you don't know what it's like to be a child in a world that has language and access for people groups who were previously unnamed or unrecognized, let alone offered the beginnings of equity and inclusion. So be gentle with each other. Be gentle with yourself. You can learn your way to leading this conversation, but mostly by listening first. Facts, knowledge, and opinion will likely hinder or harm more than welcome an exchange. They're not unimportant; they may simply not hold the highest value or be the best place to start.

I want to invite you to decide in advance of this conversation that it requires a trusting and safe relationship first. This is not a topic to be debated. It is people. Identity is people. Relationship with people is the way of God, and we see it lived out in the person of Jesus and empowered by the Holy Spirit in us, today. Furthermore, to build the relationship necessary to have a faith-based conversation about identity, we need the very strong foundation of the gospel.

As you get into this book, it may feel like it takes a long time to get into the conversation about identity. You may begin to wonder when I will land the plane, make some concrete statements, or even offer a list of how to go about getting it right. I get that. If only that manual existed for every tough conversation we get to have with kids! But because this is a *get to* conversation, we need to honor the one who defines our identity first: Jesus. So we will start with Jesus, and start with a cornerstone of gospel truth that will hold up under the weight of the identity conversation. I will spend some time equipping for a better conversation about the gospel so that we might have a better conversation about identity. And those two simply cannot be had in reverse. The gospel comes first.

I know you are bringing questions to this conversation. I know the tension that you may be experiencing: the kind of tension that started for me in my inability to reconcile what Jesus says with how our theology sometimes plays out (I was fifteen years old the first time that happened). And I know the reality that you, and the kids you love, are experiencing around emerging gender identities, sexual identity, racialization and marginalization, and the wrestling that comes with holding on to our faith tightly while looking real people in the eye. Real people who may identify differently than you do. Real people who experience the world differently than you do. Real people who are loved by God just as much as you are.

So while I understand that you might find it helpful for me to resolve some of that tension, I cannot promise that I will. I can't even promise that it won't get worse as you choose to engage in this conversation and do the work of exchanging thoughts, ideas, and questions with others, including your kids. I can only help you set the big rocks in place so that you have something to stand on as you navigate the identity conversation. I cannot answer all your questions, because every child is unique. You and I are unique. Our stories play a part in how we experience and express our identities. And while we may not have had the freedom to navigate this conversation the way that our kids can today, we get to have it now.

Parents and others who care for children, above all else, and before we go any further, please pray. Pray for deep breaths, for your shoulders to drop, for your heart to be softened. Pray for discernment and wisdom as you begin to have conversations with others. Pray for compassion like Jesus as you talk not only about identity but also about real people with real stories and real truths about who they are and how they show up in the world. Pray for those you know who are struggling to have this conversation well and those who need Jesus to join them at their table. And pray that the Holy Spirit would lead you in all that you say. May you have more questions than answers as you begin. Be ready to ask lots of questions as you consider how the ideas in this book connect with your context, whether at home, at church, or in the wider world.

My hope is that you feel equipped to *begin* the conversation with curiosity and invitation rather than go into it armed with answers. My prayer for you is that your eagerness to resolve the tension would be overwhelmed by your desire to share the love of Jesus with all people, even if that's the more difficult path, or possibly counter to how you have been following Jesus until now. My desire is for this generation of kids to experience the transformational life, love, and power of Jesus and the presence of the Holy Spirit because they know they are invited, included, and welcome in the kingdom of God. May they find their identity in Jesus so that they may fully know *the me they were made to be.*

1

HOW DO YOU
SHARE MANGO?

I was eleven months and three days into my first job as a kids' pastor when I realized it was time to quit. Ever feel like quitting? No? Just me? Hmm.

I had been sharing about Jesus at bedtime with my youngest child for at least a month, expecting that obviously she would want to give her life to Jesus, and obviously she was ready. I had talked about the joy of knowing Jesus and how he had changed my life—how his love was special and he gives good gifts. My daughter was smart and had been hearing the stories of Jesus' love and miracles her whole life. She had heard her older sister's baptism testimony and heard me teach every Sunday. Surely she understood the commitment and the choice to follow Jesus. She was already five years old, and the clock was ticking (you know the one: the clock that ticks away the seconds as if there were a moment where a child toggles from innocent to doomed without salvation). I was convinced that if I couldn't lead my own kid to Christ, I should definitely disqualify myself from ministry.

I walked into her room on that fateful night, and she told me she didn't want me to tuck her in anymore. *Is Daddy available?* Duly offended, I asked, "Why can't I tuck you in?" She told me I talked about Jesus too much, and she didn't want to hear about him anymore. "I don't want to talk to Jesus," she said. As my resignation letter began to write itself, I told her I'd be back in a month and I'd see if her dad was available until then. In hindsight, I likely needed the month to talk to Jesus more than she needed a month to not talk to me.

I spent the long summer days of that month preparing for eight weeks of church day camp, where I hoped to invite other people's kids to have a relationship with Jesus. I rehearsed all the ways to make the invitation irrefutable, how to lavish God's love on other people's kids, and how a relationship with Jesus is the best decision of their lives. You can imagine, then, how those thirty days felt: Ironic. Painful. Confusing.

Exactly one month later, I peeked around the threshold of her door as she peeked over her covers, rolled her eyes, and asked, "Has it been a month already?" Apparently, five-year-olds have tenacious memories when required.

"I just have one question," I said as I cautiously approached her and perched on the end of her bed. "Why don't you want to talk to Jesus?"

"You told me that if I let Jesus into my life, he would change everything. And I don't want him to change anything," she replied. "I like my room, my toys, my friends, my home, and my family, and I don't need anything."

I realized what I had done wrong. I had told her *my* story instead of stepping into hers. I had tried to convince a tiny human that she needed Jesus and that he would change everything if she let him in. And that she needed him to do that—except she didn't even understand the word *need*. It was like handing a five-year-old a whole mango, skin and all, and saying, "Take a bite."

And think of what would happen if she did: maybe she'd get a trace of the sweet nectar, but mostly she would get a mouthful of tough, leathery skin. Even if she could cut her way through the fruit, she'd likely hit the big, hairy pit that runs the length of the fruit and crush the golden pulp in the process. If she could manage to get the fruit off the pit but ended up cutting against the grain, it would likely floss her teeth like celery.

GETTING TO THE GOOD PART

Fruit where I'm from isn't like a mango. I grew up in Ontario, Canada, in a little city just outside the Mennonite villages of the region. I've got Mennonite roots myself. The food we ate was either grown or made by my mom, or it was grown or made by the nearby farmers. Sausage, potatoes, all manner of baking and pickling, and fruit—whatever grew locally and could be canned (even watermelon—don't ask). You may have guessed, but mango is not indigenous to the Great White North. And to be honest, I can't tell you if mangoes were in our grocery stores or markets when I was a child. But they definitely weren't in the aisles I walked with my mother. Those aisles were filled with peaches, cherries, apples, and almost any other tree fruit that you can just sink your teeth into. Eating those local fruits is easy. You just take a bite and eat around the pit.

But mangoes aren't like that. You can't just sink your teeth into a mango. If I wanted to help my daughter out, I *could* hand her a knife and some instructions. I could give her the mango and a list of how-to videos about the best, easiest, and most interesting ways to cut a mango. I could tell her about all the ways I've enjoyed a mango: in the Caribbean and the Philippines, right off the skin, in a salad or stir-fry, in a cake or sorbet . . . I'm sure that would help her understand *why* I love mango so much. It might even make her feel like she might want to try mango. But all she'd be able to say after any of this is, "My mummy really loves mango." I still wouldn't have given her anything she could chew on.

We do that, don't we? "You would love mango. You should try it." We share recipes and offer opinions and ideas. We share reels of people seemingly making magic out of mango. But I wonder what a difference it would make if we flipped the whole thing inside out and just fed someone. I wonder what I would learn about what others taste and see if I didn't tell them what they would taste and see before they even put a morsel in their mouth.

I want to watch them take a bite and let the juice hit their taste buds. I want to see their eyes light up and an involuntary look of delight wash over their face. I want to hand them the juicy fruit and let them finish it while I cut up the second half and set it in front of them. If I want someone to love mango, I want to remove every possible reason for them to say no to trying it. I want to make it easy to understand why I love it so much. We have plenty of time for cooking lessons later. But first. Take a bite.

We often fail to do this with Jesus.

When we talk about the gospel, we often start with the hairy pit of this world and all the ways to avoid it (yet spend most of our time talking about it). We warn people of the bitter skin and the trouble with getting to the good part. We explain why it's hard to crack open and why they might not like it. We even tell them what they might be doing wrong as they try to get into it. And to be blunt, though we say that Jesus' story is good news, we start with all the bad stuff that put him on the cross. We say he will make everything right, but we spend most of our time complaining about all that is wrong with the world.

And we are quick to call out all the reasons a person needs Jesus—just look at their mess! Surely their need is clear. But one's sins aren't—or shouldn't—be the only reason one needs Jesus. At least, I don't think my flaws or the ways I have fallen short are the only measure of my need. Sin defines my need for grace, my need for a Savior, and the distance between me and God. Sin tells you I am human, but it doesn't tell you my deep need for Jesus. Maybe in part. But not in full.

I need Jesus in order to know who I truly am. I need a relationship with Jesus through his Holy Spirit to understand God's glorious plan for my one life. I need Jesus to transform me by the power of his name from what I am by my own strength to who I am because of who he is. The more I look like Jesus, act like Jesus, follow Jesus, pattern my life after him, the more I get to be who I was made to be. I need Jesus because who he is unlocks God's plan for who I am—not just who I am becoming, but what is already woven into my person as an image bearer awaiting the key.

We pretend that the greatest thing that Jesus does is change us, but the greatest thing he ever did was just show up. His life, death, and resurrection are worthy of flipping inside out for others so they can sink their teeth into how much he loves them. God knows you. God thinks you're amazing. Jesus loves you, and he is the reason we know what love is. The Holy Spirit is with you. You will never walk alone. Why didn't I start there?

A FEAST WITH JESUS

The truth is, I didn't need Jesus to change my kid's life. I needed her to know him. I needed her to experience his love, his presence, and his goodness. I wanted her to love him like I do. I didn't need Jesus to flip her life inside out and change it; I needed to flip his story inside out and just invite her to feast on it.

If I had a do-over, peeking around the corner into her room that evening, I would say what Paul says in Ephesians 3:

> And so here I am, preaching and writing about things that are way over my head, the inexhaustible riches and generosity of Christ. My task is to bring out in the open and make plain what God, who created all this in the first place, has been doing in secret and behind the scenes all along. Through followers of Jesus like yourselves gathered in churches, this extraordinary plan of God is becoming known and talked about even among the angels!
>
> All this is proceeding along lines planned all along by God and then executed in Christ Jesus. When we trust in him, we're free to say whatever needs to be said and bold to go wherever we need to go. So don't let my present trouble on your behalf get you down. Be proud!
>
> My response is to get down on my knees before the Father, this magnificent Father who parcels out all heaven and earth. I ask him to strengthen you by his Spirit—not a brute strength but a glorious inner strength—that Christ will live in you as you open the door and invite him in. And I ask him that, with both feet planted firmly on love, you'll be able to take in with all followers of Jesus the extravagant dimensions of Christ's love. Reach out and experience the breadth! Test its length! Plumb the depths! Rise to the heights! Live full lives, full in the fullness of God.
>
> God can do anything, you know—far more than you could ever imagine or guess or request in your wildest

dreams! He does it not by pushing us around but by working within us, his Spirit deeply and gently within us. (vv. 8–20 *The Message*)

I wish I had told her that. And while Jesus does change everything, it's only because he is the key who unlocks God's own image in us. It's only because, as Jesus changes my child, the more she looks like Jesus, and the more she looks like Jesus, the more she grows to be who she was made to be.

This is the heart of the identity conversation: Who was she made to be? I think we are so anxious to answer that question well as parents that we forget that the answer is more than one thing. My daughter's salvation did not answer that question fully. But her answer to mine began to reveal who she is, how she learns, what she's hearing and thinking, and that my questions were more about me than they were about her.

Good conversations about identity are rooted in good conversations about a very good gospel. Getting clear about what the gospel is—and sometimes more importantly, what it isn't—is the foundation upon which one's understanding of who they were made to be stands. Because if we are going to say "made to be," we have to start with the Maker. And God is good. When God made people, God said it was very good. And Jesus is our good news. So let's start there.

The point was never that Jesus would change my daughter's life. The only point, ever, is that Jesus Christ is the same yesterday, today, and forever. And that is enough, and it is a feast. He is who he is regardless of who I am, and he does change everything, but only because he loves us. Because Jesus is Love. Because Jesus is Lord. Jesus is the Son of the living God. He is King. He is healer. He is lion and lamb, shepherd and friend, gentle and kind, good and right, present and knowing. He is compassion. He is the only way, the truth, and the life. He is everything. And you are invited to his feast.

If I truly want you to love mango, why wouldn't I just serve it to you? I want to make it easy to understand why I love it so much, but I also want you to try it on your own, to ask questions, even to share it with someone else. I don't need you to love it the way I do; it would just be such a shame if no one ever introduced you to it. We have plenty of time for cooking lessons, banter about favorite varietals, and stories of getting into it later. But first. Take a bite.

2

WHAT DO YOU LOVE
(LIKE I LOVE MANGO)?

What do you love like I love mango?
What do you wish everyone loved as much as you do? If they only knew how delicious it was . . . If only you could prepare it for us, then we might love it like you do. What is one thing that you tell everyone about? That story that your bestie has heard a thousand times but lets you tell again because they love how your face lights up when you talk about it? As you can tell, I love mango. Like, I really love mango. But it wasn't always that way. In fact, there was a time in my life when I didn't even know about mangoes.

At the ripe old age of twentysomething, I moved to downtown Toronto. To be clear, there is nothing at all similar about my hometown and Toronto. Perhaps they have as much in common as the years 1852 and 1996. But I was a little girl who grew up too fast and resented childhood for all the ways it deprived me of grownup opportunities (this included a great disdain for "the kids' table"). So I arrived in a big city with big dreams only to find myself feeling like a little girl with few street smarts: lost, unfamiliar, and alone.

Growing up too fast meant that I hadn't spent much time playing. Yet here I was, at the epicenter of entertainment, excited to jump in but not sure where to begin. I wandered into a bookstore, and wouldn't you know, a beautiful, colorful book jumped out at me. It looked like a children's book; the title was written in crayon surrounded by doodles, but it was, indeed, written for grownups—grownups like me who needed to be reintroduced to play, to whimsy, and to creativity. It was called *Succulent Wild Woman* by SARK (Susan Ariel Rainbow Kennedy). And it was the perfect instruction manual for my new beginning.

On several pages, there were lists of how-to instructions for fun activities. And there, somewhere early on in the adventure, was a how-to that sounded outlandish to this Mennonite: How to Eat a Mango. There were three simple instructions:

1.   Get naked.
2.   Get in the bath.
3.   Get into it.

It seemed easy enough. Except I didn't even know what a mango looked like, and the internet wasn't nearly as useful then as it is now. But surely one of the fruit stands in China-town would have what I needed. Even that wasn't as easy as I imagined—I literally had to read the sign to know which fruit was a mango. Because I had never seen or tasted mango. And no one had ever introduced it to me, let alone shared one with me.

Have you ever noticed how we rarely order a menu item for which we can't at least somewhat predict the flavor profile? We are willing to try new things, but we often measure the cost of the experiment and generally want to taste someone else's dish before committing to it ourselves.

But I digress.

So, here's this young woman, desperately wanting to get into a mango and no idea how. Alone. In her bathtub.

After making a mess of that poor fruit and getting covered in its sticky juice in the process, I turned to the experts. I watched Martha Stewart skillfully flip one inside out and eat the golden pulp right off the skin on TV. And I decided that it might be worth asking a chef friend of mine to show me how to cut a mango.

If you're anything like me, wanting to get into something but not sure where to begin, I wonder: Wouldn't you rather have someone flip it inside out for you than let you fight for it, struggle, or walk away, having lost interest?

Everybody has a mango. What's yours? What's something you tell everyone about and think everyone should try? Because the gospel is a lot like mango for me. We could share recipes, play videos of the best way to cut it, eat it, or cook it . . . But food just tastes better around a table with friends, doesn't it? It's amazing how it matters so much less what you're eating than whom you eat it with. To whom do you long to *serve* your mango? More to the point: To whom are you being invited to tell your story?

I was recently told by a colleague, "I love the way you love Scripture. How did you get to a place where you can't talk about it without smiling?" And I told her, "The same way I got to talking about my affection for mango: one juicy bite at a time."

I told her that I think the Bible is juicy and delicious, and that I experience it the way I do mango: inside out and messy. I want to devour it—stick my face in it, let it fill me.

To me, the Bible is the most lavish love letter ever written. Even Leviticus—maybe even especially Leviticus! Imagine

God, who always believed we were able, always believed we could, always making a way to share presence and be in relationship! A God who never thought 613 (give or take) rules was too much for God's people because they got God if they made room for holiness. A God who promised to show up if we could just create the space to be filled, a God who has always believed in us way more than we've believed in God. A God who has made a way for us to turn and return, over and over, because relationship with us has always been God's desire. The way I see it, the Bible is a love letter about a God who chooses us over and over again.

Have we lost the longing to tell the magnificent story of God's miraculous love? Have we forgotten that the whole of Scripture reminds us that this love is for everyone, and that withholding it is an *us* problem, not a *them* problem? Have we decided that the seats at our table have place cards for some, not all? Or have we left an empty seat just in case someone new receives the invitation and actually shows up?

Above all else, when you sit at my table, I want you to know that God is love, Jesus is what God is like, Scripture is a love letter, and the Spirit whispers love over you day after day. And that who you are is beloved, invited, delightful, creative, chosen, seen, accepted. Because you are loved. And you are welcome to this conversation. It's sweet, it's juicy, and it's sometimes paired with a spicy side dish.

Friends, let's pull our chairs up to the table. Imagine a feast where everyone is invited, everyone is welcome, and everyone is curious because everyone brings something to share. Is it possible for us to understand that if everyone is not at the feast, we miss out on something and we miss out on each other? Who we are is meant to reflect who the Creator is, and we miss out on some of God without the radical hospitality of this table. This table—where we are all known by God, loved by Jesus, and led by the Holy Spirit, where we all remember that each of us is made in the image of God—has a seat for you, and a seat for me. Invite all your friends because there is room. Let's say grace and dig in.

3

BEFORE WE GET INTO IT

Whenever I give a talk or have a conversation about identity, I notice some consistency in the questions that many would like to have answered under this chapter heading. Most questions are around theology or ideology, and most folks are asking me to share an opinion. The problem isn't the questions themselves, but rather the expectation that these questions are the correct ones to be asking and should frame the conversation we are going to have. (I'm not a fan of the word *should*. You should know that now.)

Many of us come to conversations about identity with working assumptions: assumptions footed in theological opinions, assumptions that there is a right or wrong way to have this conversation, and assumptions about what needs to be addressed and, moreover, where we, the church, need to land at the end of the conversation. These assumptions prompt questions that can make us into "yeah, but" listeners. *Yeah, but what about . . . ?* Moreover, "yeah, but" listeners spend a lot of energy listening for the answer to the question they think everyone is dying to ask or they feel needs to be answered, and as a result, they may miss the conversation altogether. If you have some of those questions, I am going to ask you to park them for now. Maybe you want to jot them down so that they don't distract you. And I am going to invite you to be expectant of a Holy Spirit who wants to meet with you, sit with you, listen to your questions, hold you as you wrestle, and speak to you as you invite her to draw near.

With this in mind, here are some party rules for the conversation to which you are invited:

1. There is no necessary connection between a conversation about identity and a conversation about same-sex (or any) marriage. I can see how you get there—I've gone there—but I'm hoping we can have a different conversation, a conversation about how we have the conversation in the first place, and how we lead kids, youth, and one another to find ourselves in God's story first. Today, kids ask bigger questions, more questions, and deeper questions about identity long before they consider marriage. They're also asking questions about identity at presexual ages. It is important to remember that *sexual identity and gender identity are not the same*. Sexual identity, in part, has to do with a person's sexual orientation (or attraction) and their sexual expression. Sexual identity usually begins to take shape around puberty. Gender identity, however, has to do with an individual's experience of their gender *regardless of their biological attributes*. Gender identity often emerges in early childhood and is unrelated to sexuality. For the sake of a generation that does not confuse these facets of identity, pay attention to how your biases or opinions may conflate the two. They are not the same thing. So let's sit with kids and each other in this formational space and not draw lines between the myriad dots on this landscape.

2. On that note, the word *identity* does not exclusively apply to sexuality or gender. Although it may feel like it at times, it has not been hijacked or usurped of a fuller meaning.

For centuries we have labeled people by parts of their identity and accordingly made decisions about their invitation to participate fully with the world around them (not to mention their invitation to participate in the gospel). People with disabilities. People who are not Caucasian. People with neurodivergence. People with illnesses or limps or from a lower socioeconomic strata than we are comfortable with. People with addictions or a prison record or who are divorced. Identity is a kaleidoscope. Everyone wants theirs to be held up to the light; it's prettier that way. Let's work hard to let identity be everything that it is, not only the parts with which you or others may struggle.

3. If you've met one person who identifies differently from you, you've met one person who identifies differently from you. Kind of like if you've met one Christian, you've met one Christian—we won't always agree, interpret Scripture, or interact with God the same way. I will talk about different groups of people, but they are still unique individuals within a community that shares common unity. When we dip our toes in the pool of identity, we are asking God to invite us into sacred space, where God alone knows the essence of *imago Dei* (God's own image) that God alone knit into that very beautiful person. I will work hard not to limit how God sees any of us.

4. Identity is not an issue to be solved; it's a wonder to behold. It's a person or people to be loved. It's God's image in each human, and we get to love God more by looking for God's image in others. Until we can see each person as a purposeful reflection of God's image, we are not ready to consider the cost of the alternative: an "us versus them" conversation. I will not be having an us-versus-them conversation.

5. Love can be experienced only when a person feels safe. Choosing to love others includes creating a safe space for them

to show up authentically and not in fear of your reaction, of no welcome, of exclusion, or of not having what they need once they choose to be brave and come through the doors. When these fears are realized, the tension is felt by both you and the one in front of you: when the need to hold your position overwhelms your need to hold space for them, or when there is only space for one right answer, safety is often sacrificed. Having boundaries is important. Making space to define boundaries for ourselves is the beginning of creating safe space. Agency and consent matter at every age. My hope is to equip and inspire you to have conversations that create safe space to ask questions, to wonder, and to not know. It's okay to not know how to answer every question. "I don't know" is a very good answer when it's an honest one.

6. I use the names of God, Jesus, and the Holy Spirit relatively interchangeably. They are three in one, yet I have had unique interactions with each person of the Trinity. God is in community with Godself, which includes Jesus and the Holy Spirit, and models what community looks like as a result. I was raised to believe that God is male in all forms (Father and Son seem obvious), but I came to a crossroads early in my life when I was told that I was made in the image of God. Surely God in all forms is not male or female in our earthly understanding. In the last couple of years, I have begun to use *she* and *her* pronouns for the Holy Spirit for several reasons, but specifically because the nouns for spirit, or breath, in the original biblical text languages are primarily feminine or neuter. This is just an explanation, not an invitation to debate how I got there, as these pronouns show up in the pages of this book. Using feminine pronouns in this way can also help children understand from a young age that girls and women, too, are image bearers.

7. This conversation may raise some unexpected questions for you, maybe even some pain or confusion. You may have some labels stuck to you. Ones that you did not choose for yourself and are not names given to you by your Creator. It's okay that you need this book too. It's okay to evaluate who you say you are as you invite others to do the same. You, too, get to slough off what you need not carry or what has been put on you by anything other than love.

8. This is a messy conversation. Sticky puddles seem to find me wherever I go (I may also go looking for them), but in this case, I am inviting you to join me in this beautiful mess.

4

REDEFINING NEED

Before we get into this beautiful, messy, complex conversation about identity, we need to start with the gospel. If you love Jesus, you may well understand why you need Jesus. And it may seem obvious to you while it may not be to others. It also may not be obvious that one needs Jesus. The word *need* itself is fraught with working assumptions that I have learned can hinder the sharing of the gospel perhaps more often than it helps. Take my daughter, for example: I believed wholeheartedly (still do) that she needs Jesus. I believe we all need Jesus. But what she needs him for is a conversation she gets to have with him.

I need Jesus in order to know who I truly am. I need Jesus to speak truth over me about who I am, how much I am loved, and how I am part of God's family, filled with the Holy Spirit, entrusted with gifts to be used to further the kingdom. I am who God says I am first. And in order to unlock the voice of the Spirit within, I need Jesus. Otherwise, I am only who I say I am or who others say I am, and I miss out on God's plan for me. Still, the beauty of the gospel is that I *get to* choose. I get to choose to say yes to Jesus, to listen, to follow his ways, to believe him about how I am seen, known, loved, led with a purpose on purpose for a purpose. I also get to choose to ignore all that. I get to choose to try my way, make mistakes, define myself according to, well, whatever I want. But my choices do not change who God says I am. I can choose to walk in what God says or I can choose to walk on my own. I can also choose both, and sometimes, with a lot of prayer, these choices run parallel.

But not everything about who I am is a choice. So while I am choosing to follow Jesus, I am also listening for the way, the truth, and the life that God planned for me because "all the days ordained for me were written in your book before one of them came to be" (Psalm 139:16). God knows. And this is good news. So the way God knows me also has to be good news.

In a time when there is much to be afraid of, we need to be really careful when we read Scripture with kids and interpret God's Word with kids to ensure that the news is always good. The story isn't always delightful. There are difficult, gruesome tales (including Jesus' death on the cross) that can incite fear in kids. But there is a big difference in being afraid of God and fearing God. And if we don't get that right, we risk getting the gospel wrong. In Psalm 139:14, many translations say that we are "fearfully and wonderfully made." That does not sound like good news unless you dig into the language. A synonym for *fearfully* could be *awfully*—also unhelpful. But the word *fearfully* in this context is better understood as *reverently, awe-filled, inspired, extraordinary*. You were made wonderfully, extraordinarily, reverently, to be filled with awe, wonder, and reverence for the Designer. That is who you are. And how we see ourselves is one of the pillars that hold up the extraordinary nature of the gospel.

What is good news about Jesus dying? That whole story of torture, loneliness, abuse—why would he do it? We especially wonder such things every Easter. He did it because you are worth it. Because of who you are (wonderful, extraordinary, inspired), God did absolutely everything within their power (God's, Jesus', and Spirit's, as One) to call you back to your identity: child of God, worthy of love, made in the image of the Maker. A good conversation about identity has to start with a very good gospel.

While I was overseas on a mission trip serving kids and families living in poverty, my ignorance caught me off guard. I mistakenly thought I was the hero (it's Jesus, guys—it's always Jesus, just to be clear). I thought they needed Jesus because they were marginalized and deprived of basic human necessities. I mean, I thought they needed *me*, if I'm honest. But did I also think Jesus would snap his fingers and give those kids a roof *if they would just believe*? I knew this wasn't the goal or the gospel, so how do we explain their passion for Jesus *and* their cardboard bedrooms?

Our mission, or so I thought, was to lead kids to a good gospel, no matter their circumstances. And boy, did that feel important. It wasn't until I sat in my car in the church parking lot on my first day back to work after the trip that I buckled under the weight of my privilege. I had to travel to the other side of the world to figure out that some kids need shoes, food, and water, not Jesus (they already knew, loved, and served him). How would I tell the kids I serve in my local context that they need Jesus when most have never needed (or wanted for) anything? What about the kids who are coming to church but growing up in homes where Jesus isn't the Lord? Or the ones who have all the Sunday school answers but don't understand why it matters? And for the ones who have heartbreaking needs, how would I explain that Jesus is the way, but he's not a magic wand?

What does the word *need* even mean?

I asked Jesus that question. And just so we are clear, some answers are about as easy to untangle as a shoelace tied by a toddler. Sometimes I ask Jesus questions expecting him to answer them the way I would. So the time an answer takes is directly proportionate to my willingness to be wrong, to be corrected, and to unlearn. Jesus and I have had such conversations while hiking or driving, kneeling or doodling. And this question needed more time than I wished it needed, and a lot of unlearning.

I started by taking a good, hard look at the familiar ways we talk about the gospel with kids. Each of them seemed to come up short. The images and words may have been true, but were they helpful for children? Two months and countless whiteboard mind maps later,[1] I realized the first truth that would change everything about how I share the gospel: *The gospel is true all the time.* Obviously this isn't revolutionary, but it was a handle to grab on to while I wrestled with God. The gospel tells the truth about who we are and about who God is no matter where we are in our story. It is the way through our story, but it is also the way our story was meant to be crafted. Even when you don't understand it. Even when it doesn't yet make sense. Even when life is hard, even when life is peaceful, the gospel is always good. Even when you don't need anything to change. Even when you don't understand your need. And this is where I got stuck again. How do we use the word *need* with kids in a way they can understand, and in a way that invites them into God's story? Do we share the gospel with kids in a way that sounds delightful, loving, good?

The language we use to tell the stories of Scripture is the difference between a history lesson and a love letter. We can tell individual stories about how God showed up for people a long time ago; or we can tell the story of a loving God who has been showing up for people forever, a God who continues to show up and love us today. And the truth of the love written between every line of Scripture is the one thing that never changes. So, what if I could share the gospel the same way for all kids, regardless of circumstance, life stories, ability, or perceivable need? While I sat in that parking lot, I realized that I had been talking about two very different Jesuses: one for kids in squatter communities and another for kids in privileged communities.

I had to ask myself: Why was it easier for me to talk about Jesus on that mission trip, even with kids who spoke minimal English, than it was to invite kids in my neighborhood to follow Jesus? This is what my first whiteboard mind map revealed:

1. Little shared language meant our language had to shift. The words got simpler. Sentences got shorter. And I got to the point quicker.
2. My assumption that I was bringing the gospel to these children was overturned by their worship-ready posture. Once I realized that the Holy Spirit had begun a conversation with them long before I got there, it got easier: all I had to do was join in.
3. They were hungry. And thirsty. And poorly clothed. So we took care of those needs first so that they were equipped physically to participate spiritually. And isn't that just like Jesus, to meet our needs? I mean, that's why they're called *needs*.

Need brought me to my knees again. What in the world do the kids in my neighborhood actually *need*? Yes, I know, they need Jesus. But what are they lacking without him that they are desperate for, and seeking? And in her gentleness and kindness, the Spirit leaned in and whispered, "Tell them the truth about who they are." In that moment, I heard another important truth.

I decided to start there: who they are matters to their understanding of whose they are. I started yet another mind map. I put IDENTITY at the center of my whiteboard, and I began to see that language, once again, was a hindrance. Simple words were sufficient. In our desire to teach kids biblical, sacred language, we had somehow forgotten how to define those important words.

What if we decided that plain language, easy access, and inclusion in the story is the beginning of very good news? It's hard to get excited about good news if you don't understand it. And it's hard to join a party that you're not sure you were invited to in the first place. So let's make the celebration clear and be sure to leave no one out.

I filled that whiteboard with all the things that need to be included to make the gospel the gospel. What could I *not* leave out? Every time I added a word that I was sure wouldn't come up on a playground or in the schoolyard, I looked for three ways to say it differently in everyday terms. Words like *sin, redemption, sacrifice, atonement*; even the words *broken, lost, separated*. These are scary words, friends. For children below the "age of reason" (typically eight years and younger), or even for older concrete thinkers and learners, *broken* can mean many things. For example, broken bones, broken family, broken toys or favorite things. But one thing broken can't be is good. While you and I understand the word metaphorically (and perhaps even more appropriately, like breaking in a horse or a new pair of shoes), we can't make this assumption with kids. Likewise, the idea of being lost or separated fosters fear within a child. If perfect love casts out fear (1 John 4:18), and if God is love, fear cannot be the vehicle by which we introduce kids to love or goodness.

We do this to kids all the time: we use biblical words that are not everyday vernacular for most adults, let alone today's kids. What do we even mean when we use them? We need to decide. This is part of equipping ourselves for a gospel conversation *for the sake of an identity conversation*.

- *Sin* is anything that separates us from the presence of God. Sin is a choice we make that does not show God love or share God's love. Sin is a choice that serves us but hurts Jesus. When we perceive something as sin, how do we respond? We look to Jesus. What were the choices he made? What were the instructions he gave in difficult situations? And how did he handle tricky passages of scripture when asked? From what I can find in the pages of his story, Jesus moved toward the sinner, the person who was distant from God, and he sat down. And he didn't start the conversation by calling the person out for a thing they may not have understood was hurting them. When we talk about sin, I think we need to focus on the person and to make it compelling to want to close the distance between us and God. Salvation isn't *not sinning*; relationship with Jesus is.

- Without the context of the cross, the words *redemption*, *sacrifice*, and *atonement* are rich words that put a barrier between you and the one in front of you. And I am suggesting that before the cross can make sense, Jesus needs to make sense. We have to want kids to know Jesus before they can understand what happened to him. When we handle this well, we can foster empathy and compassion in kids as they understand that Jesus made a way for us to know God.

- *Broken*, *lost*, and *separated* are everyday words that kids hear in many contexts. However, after the work of building relationship with Jesus, it can feel scary that such things could happen to us or to our friendship with Jesus. To tell a child that they are "broken" can be heard very literally. Is that how Jesus sees a child, or is that how we scare a child into "needing" Jesus? Having lost one of my kids in Hollywood Studios when they were five years old, I can confirm that the word *lost* is downright terrifying. And *separated* is a complicated word, especially for kids who come from a "broken" home. (See what I did there? Please do be careful with the words you choose.)

After I made many, many mind maps, I invited others into the conversation. And we came up with a few truths that would stick and words that would invite, no matter how we tell the story: of who God is, who I am, and our need for Jesus. And two months later, it boiled down to three sentences: God made you. God's plan is for you. Jesus is the only way.

God made you. You are amazing, and God delights in you. God made you for a purpose designed long before you even began your adventure in this life. God made you to play a role in the kingdom that only you can fulfill. God fills you with everything you need, sees all that you can be, and loves you as you are today.

God's plan is for you (not against you). It's designed for you and with only you in mind to live it out the way that God made you to. God's plan for you is already in you, knit into your being, which means God also made you able to live it out. It may not be easy. It may not always be fun. But God's plan is always good and for you, with you, in you.

Jesus is the only way. He's the only way to unlock God's plan for you and hear directly from God about how and why you are made just as you are. Jesus is the only way to truly know who you are and why you're here. Jesus makes you a child of God. And when that's your identity, everything else pales in comparison. As a child of God, you do not have to know the way, and you are not alone. The Holy Spirit is with you, listens to you, talks with you, leads you, holds space for you. She knows the way.

In a culture that is urging our kids to define their identity and offering them a buffet of options, they are grappling with who they truly are and feeling that they need to know. And they *do* need to know! They need to know that *who I truly am is hardwired into me because I want to know the one in whose image I was created.*

Please hear me: The cross matters. The fullness of the gospel matters. Explaining sin matters. But that's just not where we need to begin. Our kids need a good God with a good plan and a way back to God's presence. Because, let me tell you, the enemy gets plenty of headlines, but he just doesn't get to be the protagonist in this story. Because God was, is, and always will be, good. And our kids *need* good news.

In light of 1 Peter 3:15—"You must worship Christ as the Lord of your life. And if someone asks about your hope as a believer, always be ready to explain it" (NLT)—maybe these questions will help you wrestle with the language of the gospel for the sake of the kingdom:

- What words do you use that may be a hindrance to the listener? Are there any words that may feel like insider lingo? Could those words wait for the relationship to grow?

- Where have you made Jesus a superhero instead of a savior? Words like *rescuer* may make false promises for little ones who don't understand metaphor or who think, for example, that if he rescues them from unsafe situations, they'll automatically wake up in a safe home. I told my daughter that Jesus would make "all things new" when she was five, and she wanted nothing to do with him because she liked her life exactly as it was!

- Does your gospel story deal more with sin management than identity? While Jesus does deal with our sin, and repentance is essential, the gospel is transformative and relational, not transactional. Does your gospel invite kids into a relationship that goes both ways? Does it tell of a good God who loves them no matter what? Does your gospel tell a child who they are in Jesus?

5

SHARPENING YOUR KNIFE
(TO GET INTO IT)

For Christian parents, conversations about identity often start with the Bible, and while the Bible is a great place to start, we need to understand our relationship to Scripture and how that shapes how we talk about it with others. So before digging into verses that prove whatever point we're trying to make, we need to get really clear about the role that Scripture plays in our lives.

I know you love the Bible. I know that it matters deeply to you and defines your walk with Jesus. But I also know how easy it is for what other disciples say *about* God's Word to influence how we read it. And I know how desperately you want a conversation about identity in Christ to go well for those you love, serve, walk with. We long to know God intimately and to hear from the Holy Spirit personally, and we want that for others too. So how do we engage with Scripture expectant that the Spirit will speak and drown out the voices of influence that may hinder clarity?

Our relationship with the Bible plays a significant role in how we present Scripture to others. How we see it, handle it, and interact with it affects our narrative and even our relationships with those who lean into the conversation, not to mention the impact on our relationship with Jesus. Hebrews 4:12 says that "the word of God is alive and active. Sharper than any double-edged sword, it penetrates even to dividing soul and spirit, joints and marrow; it judges the thoughts and attitudes of the heart." When we anticipate the Word as active and alive, we can also anticipate that we have something to learn from others who are seeing, handling, and interacting with Scripture. I believe I have something to learn *from the Holy Spirit* when I choose to read Scripture with other Jesus followers. If I decide that a verse or passage can mean only one thing, or that a rule or law in Scripture has not changed over time, we deny the very breath of the Spirit in its pages. What are we to do with Leviticus 19:28's instructions regarding tattoos and piercings, for example? What are we to do with Leviticus in general if we pick and choose which parts of Scripture are allowed to breathe and which ones aren't?

Read Scripture with others. Expect the Holy Spirit to speak. Get excited about what you might learn from another believer's reading of a text and how they might see or hear what has not been revealed to you. And delight in how God uses you in the same way for others. Be open to a fuller conversation because you anticipate the Spirit to be present and you believe that the Word of God is both alive and active.

There are a few things to keep in mind as we consider this deeply personal relationship:

1. Strengthening our relationship with Scripture is the same as developing any healthy discipline. In the same way that a healthy relationship with your body may start with a walk instead of a marathon, a healthy relationship with Scripture is about committing to the work of getting to know it, giving it room to breathe, and committing to stick with it even

when it doesn't make sense, even when it is disciplining you while discipling you, even when it requires more of you than you initially intended to offer the relationship. The principles that apply here are more like "a long obedience in the same direction," as author and theologian Eugene Peterson says, than they are like a scheme to "lose weight in ninety days." A scheme is a quick-fix change that isn't about relationship, but about outcomes. Scripture is always about relationship—with it, with God, and with others.

2. If we are looking to Scripture to be a manual or a textbook, it could either let us down or make us self-righteous. Meaning, if we try to shoehorn every current circumstance into Scripture, we may have to wrestle with whether or not the shoe fits. The law has context. The stories have context. The needs of the people involved in the stories were real, and they were specific. We can learn from them, but we must do more than simply transfer them to today. As learners of Scripture, we can decide to care more about what God has for us, today, in the pages, than to simply transfer what they say to the moment we are in. When we allow the Holy Spirit to breathe life into its pages, we can assume that she will speak, interpret, give way for new questions, and highlight what she has for us rather than what we need it to say to prove a point or judge other image bearers.

3. If we simply read the Bible, it makes us knowledgeable. If we interact with it, it has the power to make us holy. There is much to know about the ways of God, the people of Israel, and the followers of Jesus by reading the Bible. Many cultures respect Scripture as a historically accurate account of ancient days. And this history is so significant to our understanding of how and why and when Jesus came as he did. Yet just as a scientist does experiments to galvanize theories found among

the pages of a chemistry textbook, we are invited to live out
what the text of Scripture requires of us. Here's what I mean:
You can have two molecules of hydrogen, and one of oxy-
gen, but unless you put them together, you do not have water.
Likewise, you can read about the life of Jesus. You can even
believe that it is possible for the Holy Spirit to indwell people
when they believe in Jesus, but unless you pray and develop
a relationship with God and God's Word, it's just a theory.
The book does not transform your life. Jesus does. What if his
teachings, his walk, and his ways are actually transformative?
What if that is enough, even when life is hard, even when it
doesn't make sense, even when we don't have all the answers
for a conversation? Obedience to the text isn't meant to make
our lives hard. Obedience to the discipleship of Jesus is meant
to make our lives holy. The more we walk like him, the more
we become who we were made to be: holy. We were made for
worship, reverence, awe, wonder, blessing, and godliness. We
can read about it or become it. The choice is ours.

If we want to find a biblical example of a healthy relationship with Scripture, we need look no further than the Israelites
in the time of Ezra and Nehemiah, who had not only lost their
temple and been scattered in exile but also lost the book of
the law—their Scriptures. You know how some moments in
our lives can instantly produce an emotional reaction in us: a
child's birth, an award or accomplishment, a person of influence, a trauma? For the Israelites, it was the very sight and
sound of the book of law being opened and read:

> Ezra the priest brought the Law before the assembly, which
> was made up of men and women and all who were able to
> understand. He read it aloud from daybreak till noon as he
> faced the square before the Water Gate in the presence of

the men, women and others who could understand. And all
the people listened attentively to the Book of the Law. . . .

Ezra opened the book. All the people could see him because he was standing above them; and as he opened it,
the people all stood up. Ezra praised the LORD, the great
God; and all the people lifted their hands and responded,
"Amen! Amen!" Then they bowed down and worshiped
the LORD with their faces to the ground. . . .

They read from the Book of the Law of God, making it
clear and giving the meaning so that the people understood
what was being read. (Nehemiah 8:2–3, 5–6, 8)

What comes after this in Nehemiah is a long list of next
steps for Israel as they remembered and began to walk in the
ways of God again. And it started with confession. It started
with cleaning up their way of life. It started at the foundation, with the book of the law as their instruction manual,
not only in how to *be* the kingdom but in how to *live in*
community. The rebuilding of God's temple was a model for
the rebuilding of God's family.

Here's the good news we find in this story: Scripture is full
of do-overs.

And this is good news, because in this story we see a fun-
damental truth: God's people are a forgetful people. *We* are
a forgetful people. When we lose touch with someone, we
begin to forget what brought us together, what we loved about
hanging out, even the memories we made. The same is true for
our relationship with God. In Ezra 3 (part of the same story
as Nehemiah 8), the enduring Word shows us what happens
when we forget about our relationship with God:

And all the people gave a great shout of praise to the LORD,
because the foundation of the house of the LORD was laid.

But many of the older priests and Levites and family heads, who had seen the former temple, wept aloud when they saw the foundation of this temple being laid, while many others shouted for joy. No one could distinguish the sound of the shouts of joy from the sound of weeping, because the people made so much noise. And the sound was heard far away. (Ezra 3:11–13)

We also forget who *we* are because of who *God* is when we forget what God's Word says about both.

Two things were happening in this moment for the people of God: Some were shouting with joy because what they had heard and what they had been taught while in exile began to make sense—*we are God's chosen people*! They didn't know there was a book—all had been lost to them because they came after the fall of the temple. Others were weeping—evidence of the memory of what had been, or who they had been in community with one another. They had been at the first temple, maybe even together. They knew the way it was supposed to be, and it had been a long time. It was also an experience of what wasn't: if they had been at the first temple's completion, they would have known that the fire of the presence of God fell on the temple. And this time, the fire didn't come. So what did this say about who God is and who they were now?

The truth can be two things—and is likely more than two things in this moment with the intermingling of tears of joy and the sounds of weeping. What I find beautiful about the Israelites' relationship with Scripture is that they all knew that it mattered: the uncovering, the elevating, and the participation with the book of the law mattered, and they had a physical response to it. The way I read Scripture today can also point to my relationship with Jesus, my participation in his kingdom, and my belief in a God who *is* love. Does the relationship I have with Scripture reflect my affection for Jesus? Does reading it develop intimacy with him? Do I find myself finding myself as Jesus reveals himself through the pages of Scripture?

Are you following Scripture, or are you following Jesus? One is a way of being; the other is a way of loving. And there is room for both. Perhaps one is an experience of the other. It is impossible to know Jesus without Scripture, that is certain. But I wonder if simply reading Scripture leads to following Jesus or to just following its teachings like an instruction manual. One is like reading a map. The other is like taking the map on a walk with your best friend and deciding together which way to go. I love maps and am so curious about all the places I have yet to visit. But I cannot say much about the experience of visiting any of them until I actually journey to those places.

You may feel the urge to remind me that there are a lot of how-tos in Scripture, and I would agree. But I have learned how to follow the Word of God, Jesus Christ (John 1), by interacting with God's Word: learning his ways in Scripture, walking in his ways, then living it out in relationship with others. When our relationship with Scripture is more about figuring out what (or who) is right or wrong, we forsake relationship for rules. Staring at the map and yelling "You're going the wrong way!" while watching someone walk away isn't what the rules are for. And I just can't find permission to do so anywhere in the ministry of Jesus or the tenets he preached.

Jesus taught love above all things. If our rules, or even our following, do not look like love, patience, kindness (or any fruit of the Spirit, for that matter—for reference, see Galatians 5), we may need to revisit the map. Jesus walked. He visited people and places. He took his time so that he didn't just meet people, he made memories with those he encountered.

This is what love looks like. And when you know the way, Jesus himself, you choose relationship with people as a means to introducing others to him and then God's Word.

Here are some questions to ask yourself to help strengthen your personal relationship with the Bible:

1. Have you decided that it is a relationship? Do you need to look at your planner to make space for it, or is it a part of your life? For example, you can admire someone from afar, but until you start spending time with them, you're not in a relationship.

2. What do you expect Scripture to do for you? What is its purpose in your life? What do you hope for as you read the glorious story of God's heart to partner with us throughout history? And what do you hope to bring to each encounter with Scripture? You get to decide! You can begin with the goal in mind and fix your eyes in the direction you hope to travel with Jesus as you explore his story, together.

3. Who do you hope to become as you spend time in Scripture? You can read about plumbing and watch YouTube videos to fix a leaky faucet, but this doesn't make you a plumber. We know that reading about Jesus doesn't make us a Jesus follower. So as we find the inspiration to spend time with our Bibles, what, or who, do we hope to become as we are inspired to be more like Jesus?

4. How might reading Scripture for pleasure, for instruction, and for relationship shape you, your leadership, and your relationship with others? Second Timothy 3:16–17 says, "All Scripture is God-breathed and is useful for teaching, rebuking,

correcting and training in righteousness, so that the servant of God may be thoroughly equipped for every good work." These active verbs are possible only in the context of relationship. And notice the "so that": *so that* the servant of God may be thoroughly equipped. That's you. That's me. That's everyone we serve. That's what makes the Bible living and active. And it plays out in relationship, equipping you *thoroughly* to serve others.

5. Delighting and participating in the ways and words of Scripture will either make *you* look good or it will make *Jesus* look real. One runs the risk of saying "Look at me." The other says "Look at him." What if we get to be the generation who remembers and teaches kids to remember? Be the generation who celebrates, remembers, repeats, and imitates.

6. Are you in a desert season? Are you hungry and thirsty? The story of manna in Exodus is for us, too. God promises to meet our needs daily. God loves hearing from you every day and likely has something to say to you through the Bible every day, too. How often do you share a reel with a friend on Instagram or call your mother or text with your spouse, child, or bestie? And you wouldn't text them a reply without first reading what they'd sent first. What if we interacted with Scripture, and with the presence of the Holy Spirit, like we do with each other?

As you deepen your relationship with God, God's Word will come alive. God will speak to you through it. You will have questions, and God can answer them in the way you are wired to hear best. But you have to practice listening to understand what you're hearing. God may begin to change your mind about things you thought were in there, or ideas you felt you understood, or theologies you had adopted without interacting with the Spirit or the text. And like that time you thought you replied to a text only to find a week later that you never did, every relationship requires time, attention, mutuality, and connection. God is always ready to meet with you. God delights in you. And the presence of the Spirit is with you. What a gift! What a joy!

6

NOW WHAT? (I THOUGHT MANGOES WERE SWEET)

I wonder if maybe there is a knot in your stomach at this point. I wonder if you're feeling disoriented by an inside-out gospel, or if you're sticky from the mess of trying to get into it. I wonder if there is a knot at the end of your rope so you can hang on with me as we contend for good news amid the conversations we need to have.

I also wonder what you may need to let go of in order to grab on to that rope.

After every whiteboard mind map, every tear, every question I had for Jesus in the middle of what felt like a mess, his grace for me made space to pound my fists, grit my teeth, ask my questions, and right my wrongs along the way. He also let me take my time, even when it felt like it was taking too long. Because what I realized in the middle of that tension was that I was standing at the cross asking him to rip out of my hands whatever I shouldn't be holding on to. But what I learned was that he wanted me to unfurl my fingers, release the tension in my fists, and lay it down. Jesus invites us to choose. But there's only one way to leave it with him.

Is there an ideology you're holding on to? Sometimes, a theology, an interpretation, or a construct that feels safer to leave standing may begin to feel wobbly after conversations about identity. What happens if the foundation isn't what you thought it was? What if it isn't black-and-white after all? What if it isn't this or that, right or wrong, sin or not? The same grace that Jesus offered me in the middle of my wobbling is available in the middle of your uncertainty, no matter the source of the contention. Sometimes being "right" isn't winning. What (or whom) do you stand to lose in your need to be right, find resolve, reach a conclusion?

The tension experienced by the remnant of Israel that gathered for the rebuilding of the temple is a reminder that God has asked the family to hold things loosely before. Being willing to reconsider what we know, think, or believe isn't inherently a bad thing—in fact, just as we see in Ezra and Nehemiah, sometimes God is calling us to do this very thing. The story of the rebuilding of the temple is beautiful, but it wouldn't be possible without the prophetic picture given to Zechariah that set the stage for those moments. In Zechariah's vision, Zerubbabel, one of two men to lead Jewish exiles back from Babylon, receives the word of the Lord:

> "Not by might nor by power, but by my Spirit," says the Lord Almighty.
>
> "What are you, mighty mountain? Before Zerubbabel you will become level ground. Then he will bring out the capstone to shouts of 'God bless it! God bless it!'"
>
> Then the word of the Lord came to me: "The hands of Zerubbabel have laid the foundation of this temple; his hands will also complete it. Then you will know that the Lord Almighty has sent me to you." (Zechariah 4:6–9)

Some of the things to which we have held tightly have become mountains that need to be leveled. If the capstone can be found beneath the rubble of that which needs to fall, it is worth the work of bringing it down. In my own journey, I had to ask myself what I could do to make level ground for others to stand on and find themselves in the very good story of a very good God. Perhaps there is a mountain that needs to be leveled in order for you to develop a holy curiosity for what's on the other side. It's okay to feel a measure of uncertainty or insecurity as you stare down that mountain. Many have done the same, but we would tell you it's worth it. What's on the other side, what you can't yet see because of the mountain, is worth it. The people on the other side are worth it. You are worth it. And you are not alone.

When we feel so certain about our theological position on the subject of identity, there is often a felt tension in our conversations about identity. We tend to hold on to theological ideas because we believe they are sacred, and these ideas stand like mountains in front of us. Tension mounts as we disagree, as we argue our points and strengthen our grip on what we believe. I feel the tension when I utter the word *identity* inside the walls of churches and things dull to a hush as the air gets sucked out of the room. And I know you feel it too. I wonder if we can sit with each other no matter what side of the mountain we find ourselves on. I wonder if we can simply name the tension and acknowledge that we may not agree on how to level the mountain or even whether it needs to be leveled. But I also wonder if we can agree that the way we have this conversation about identity tells others whether they want to have a conversation with us about Jesus, let alone identity.

Our identity is, indeed, found in Jesus. Our identity is best understood as image-bearing children of God, without a doubt. But this isn't the language to start with when we are introducing people to the idea that there is a loving God who cares about who they are and how they show up in the world. And we also have to affirm, collectively, that being like Jesus matters yet will look different for each of us, since each of us is uniquely wired to reflect God's image. I mean, look at us! The Author of all creativity knows the diversity with which we each face the day. God knows how our brains work: from our bodies, our thoughts, our choices, our wonderings, and our wanderings, God isn't afraid of how differently we come to know Jesus or come to reflect him back to the world around us. Rather, it is our collective human imagination that seems to limit the possibilities of what this could look like.

What if the truest definition of identity meant that *the more I am like Jesus, the more I am the me I was made to be*? If this is true, then being me has to matter. As Christ followers, we were made to reflect the image of God to those around us through the love of Jesus, by the leading of the Spirit. This is the core of our identity. But I wonder if we decide someone is doing it wrong when their reflection is different from ours, or even different from what we thought was possible, acceptable, or even godly. Godliness matters, but I think we often have a picture in our minds of what being godly looks like. I wonder how often that picture looks like Jesus. Because of who Jesus is and how he lived his life, we don't have to define godliness beyond Jesus. As we orient our bodies toward him, we grow to be more like him—this is the way of becoming, the way of growing into who we were made to be. When my identity centers on the identity of Jesus Christ, godliness is an outward demonstration of that growth. And there will be evidence.

But we have changed our minds about the meaning of godliness before. And we will change our minds on matters of theology again. We have watched pastors and denominations change their minds quite publicly on the role of women, same-sex marriage, interracial marriage, worship styles, versions of Scripture translation, baptism, division of church and state, to name a few. And we have questioned whether they're "doing it wrong," whether their choices are "godly" on one side of their theology and the other. But who they are and their commitment to follow Jesus even to the extent of letting him change their minds is relevant and humbling. Tightly held theology does not make us godly; obedience to Jesus does.

I believe that we can disagree theologically and still be catalysts for kingdom expansion, obedient to Jesus, and useful to the Spirit. I believe that every Jesus follower gets the Holy Spirit in equal measure, and I trust the Holy Spirit to do what only she can do in and through people even when I don't understand their position. I also believe that Jesus models a beautiful example of asking hundreds of questions and invites us to do the same. I want to know more about your relationship with Jesus and your orientation toward his mission and its fulfillment in real time. And I believe that all people everywhere are invited to participate in this mission. If we want godly people on mission with us, I am confident that becoming more and more like Jesus bears a family resemblance that we will recognize in one another.

In our world, identity means many things. While the word *identity* is centuries old and can be traced back to ancient Latin, its modern usage began to rise in printed text starting only in the late 1980s.[1] (We'll dig into the etymology of *identity* later in this chapter.) The word itself has evolved in both meaning and use, and that has left some of us unsure of how we are using (or misusing) it. We often assume, however, that we all define identity in the same way. But as we dig into what we mean, and what we think we all mean, we begin to peel back the layers on a rich, multifaceted, confusing, and challenging conversation where we may not have even begun at the same starting point.

What are your working assumptions about the meaning of the word *identity*? What does it include? What does it not include? What are your theological stakes in the ground that need to be identified? What do you need to ask of others so that unspoken expectations do not become premeditated resentments?[2] If we want kids to truly know who they are—to be rooted in kingdom identity and confident children of God regardless of how they're wired or show up in the world—what do we need to let go of so that wiring doesn't get tangled with our presumed factory settings?

IDENTITY IS COMPLICATED

We might feel several tensions, and that makes this such a difficult conversation—especially if we have each individually predetermined what identity is or isn't (and assumed what we think is universal).

1. The first tension is that the word *identity* can define what makes us unique *and* what allows us to feel like we belong. This is, essentially, a tension between difference and sameness. And ultimately, the word means both. Meaning, I want to be my own person, not defined by any collective group or stereotype, but I also want to be part of something bigger than me. And that belonging is usually found in community with others with whom we share common interests or beliefs. But we want to participate as ourselves: accepted, but unique, not expected to conform.

More importantly, the word needs to mean both in order to find our identity in Jesus: I am a unique being created by

God for God's own glory, and no one can take my place in the kingdom. I am also made for community in order to know other aspects of what God is like and how God's image shows up in others. I am different from you in how God made me to do that. I also need you in order to understand how we fit together. God is in community with themselves (God, Jesus, Spirit), and I was made for community so that God would be made known.

Further, the more I choose to be like Jesus, to walk in his ways, to carry his truth, his love, his life with me, the more I get to be fully me. In other words, the more I am *the same* as Jesus, the more *uniquely different* I appear to be in the world, unlike any other image bearer. The more like Jesus I become, the more the me I was made to be is released by the power of the Holy Spirit.

2. The second tension is between what stays the same about a person throughout their life *and* what changes over time. Think ethnicity versus aging. As humans, we change throughout our lives—children become adults, bodies change, some people get married, and some become parents. Others are able-bodied but develop diseases that change their mobility while some are born with disabilities that last a lifetime. I was not a mother at eight years old; yet today, motherhood is part of my identity. Some things about us are true throughout our lifetime. Some things aren't. Identity shifts. And how we are seen versus how we see ourselves—who we are versus who we are becoming—stand in conflict with each other at different developmental intersections of our lives. But if we can understand the shifts in our own identity (and the possible confusion, pain, disorientation it all can cause), can we show mercy to those who are experiencing unexpected shifts or who are reconciling things they hoped would change that haven't?

"Always" or "never" statements often collide with our changing (or unchanging) truths. And our desires for our lives are not always fulfilled. Our desire to *be* something is not always reconciled with actually *becoming*. There is probably something you can remember wanting to be or not wanting to be when you were little. Maybe you wanted to be tall or to have blue eyes. Maybe you were racialized or marginalized because you were new or different or didn't speak English when you started school. Maybe you thought that a voice change during puberty meant you'd get a sweet girl voice instead of the raspy bark you were born with.

That was me. I thought that. No one told me voice changes were just for males. I still have the same no-I'm-not-recovering-from-laryngitis-and-it-doesn't-get-better-or-cuter lilt to my voice. You can laugh. It's funny. But kids are begging God to change or take away or heal or remove myriad things about themselves that don't change. And we can't have a good conversation with them about their identity if we don't take these things seriously. Too often we start with telling them what should or shouldn't change, when we could better start by simply listening to them and helping them understand how these things may—or may not—be a fixed part of their identity.

3. The third tension is the pull between what I know for sure and what I don't yet know. This is more internal than external, and some truths require a growth mindset, the ability to add "yet" to the end of a sentence. Some things are always true about me. Some things will not always be true. What I know for sure, and what I want every child ever to know for sure, is what is true about them according to Scripture: how God sees them and how God names them.

These truths are more about character. How I see myself may be different from how God sees me, but the more I allow

God's vision of me and for me to inform *who* I am, the more it influences *how* I am in relationship with other people and with the world around me. Scripture is full of truths about who we are as God's image bearers, how God sees us, loves us, and knows us. Pointing to these truths and allowing them to inform what is always true about each of us helps those of us who are not yet able to see others with God's eyes, listen to their stories with God's ears, or love with God's compassion for their story. (Exodus 3 is an early example of how God naming that we are seen and heard and God's heart move the Father into action and compassion for his kids.)

4. There is even tension in the language we use to explore identity: *binary* versus *nonbinary*, and this goes beyond gender. The language can seem tricky, especially if we are uncomfortable or unclear about how it applies to gender, but it's actually quite simple: *binary* is the difference between being one of two things whereas *nonbinary* can be one of many things on a spectrum. Some things are black-or-white. Many things are shades of grey. Your experience of your own identity may be quite matter-of-fact. Your experience of your own gender or sexual identity may be binary. And as clear as that was to you when you realized these truths about your identity, so is the clarity for others who identify differently from you. And sometimes the clarity is simply "I am neither." There is a tension in that for those of us who may not understand how that can be true or who find it confusing rather than clarifying. And the fact that you don't need to understand likely doesn't resolve the tension.

But the things that you didn't choose, others likely didn't either. Some of the greatest tensions have come from insisting that certain identifiers are choices when research and testimony clearly articulate that they are not. To be clear: if you do not believe you chose to be heterosexual, you cannot assume someone chooses not to be. Likewise, and in the words of clinical psychologist Mark Yarhouse, "people do not choose gender incongruence."[3] Being transgender or homosexual (or identifying one's gender or sexuality differently from the majority) may be a person's experience of sexuality *in equal measure* to your experience of being straight, even if you believe that God designed humans as heterosexual beings.

I understand the story of creation. I understand God's original design (at least to the extent that anyone can wrap one's mind around a perfect plan in a perfect place with a perfect God). I understand how beautiful it all must have been. And I understand, perhaps far better, the fall. Ever since God chose to add humanity to the story, God has also chosen to give us choice, agency, and consent in God's own story. That may be the hardest thing of all to wrap our minds around: that in order for us to experience the full measure of God's love, we had to experience the full measure of choosing to love God back. But our choice was not limited. And in the unlimited realm of choice, doubt, fear, and sin entered the story. Whether or not of our own doing, we all now live in bodies that fall short of God's original design. This is the tension: what we imagine God's intended design was versus the spectacular diversity we encounter in one another everyday. People experience myriad ways of being that may seem to be in conflict with our views of what God intended, however narrow or broad those views may be. I imagine it is better to hold this tension than to wrongly resolve it.

So can we give one another grace for experiencing shades in between what has, until recently, been understood as binary by the majority who set the agenda and generally controlled the conversation? We know that most people are heterosexual.

We know that most people are cisgender.[4] We know that most people are neurotypical, able-bodied, and unhindered by how their bodies work or communicate with their brains. Is it possible, however, that *regardless of the subject or theological argument*, your experience of binary is not everyone's? We have conceded many theological binaries that are not as we previously believed: the role of women in the church, interracial marriage, that dancing leads to sex (or does sex lead to dancing? Depends on the denomination, I guess). Different theologies, or theological constructs of interpretation, have been reimagined over time, most often because we have made mistakes, we have been abusive, and we have misunderstood or misused ancient texts. Stepping into this conversation well means approaching it with humility, recognizing that we may be wrong, or even that we may have work to do. This could allow us to better hear someone else's experience and be present with them as they navigate their questions about who and whose they are.

In order to sit well with these tensions and with each other, I suggest we embrace wonder, explore unanswered questions without the need to answer or agree, and welcome the discomfort of not knowing or having it all figured out. In this space, we get to invite God to reveal God's will before we name our own, to answer questions that are not frustrating or complicated to God, and to comfort us in our uncertainty. God's ways are not our ways. We can confidently embrace the mystery of the divine and trust that the Holy Spirit sees and hears us, has a heart of compassion for us, and walks with us. Even when we don't understand. Even when the tension seems to be too much. Even if the shift we long to see in others begins to happen in us first. When I trust the God of wonder who holds all things together, I can trust that I am a wonder too.

A PLACE OF WONDER

Wonder is the heart of childlike faith we are never meant to outgrow. Wonder allows us to sit in a place of tension, of not knowing, of curiosity. It allows us to trust God in the spaces we can't yet see or even define. This posture is key to having good conversations about identity, yet it often requires some unlearning for us as adults (and implies that we may need children to teach us).

Returning to childlikeness may be the first step for some of us—to remember what it was like to not know things and to go hunting for information, answers, and big ideas. There was a time when our imagination fueled our pursuits and who we were was "whatever we want to be!" Some of us woke up as dragons; others as princesses. Some of us woke up wondering whether we were made wrong.

Scripture defines our *identity* in one way: by our inclusion in God's family: "You are no longer foreigners and strangers, but fellow citizens with God's people and also members of his household" (Ephesians 2:19). "See what great love the Father has lavished on us, that we should be called children of God! And that is what we are! The reason the world does not know us is that it did not know him" (1 John 3:1). "You are a chosen people, a royal priesthood, a holy nation, God's special possession, that you may declare the praises of him who called you out of darkness into his wonderful light" (1 Peter 2:9). "Therefore since we are God's offspring, we should not think that the divine being is like gold or silver or stone—an image made by human design and skill" (Acts 17:29). "So in Christ Jesus you are all children of God through faith, for all of you who were baptized into Christ have clothed yourselves with Christ. There is neither Jew nor Gentile, neither slave nor free, nor is there male and female, for you are all one in Christ Jesus. If you belong to Christ, then you are Abraham's seed, and heirs according to the promise" (Galatians 3:26–29). In Scripture, there is no use for identity outside of belonging. That doesn't mean we have not come to use and mean the word *identity* in more than one way. While it seems oxymoronic, even in God's Word, identity means both communal belonging and individual uniqueness not just sociologically, but also scripturally.

Scripture talks about our unique image-bearing nature, how the hairs on our heads are counted (Matthew 10:30) and our individual days numbered (Psalm 139:16). This is highly specific and individualized, meaning God knows each of us personally. It matters that we reconcile *this* particular tension: that while our biblical understanding of identity is belonging (one big family), God's understanding of each one of us is personal and intimate.

This beautiful truth leads us to the possibility of reconciling our identity as both/and: *the more I am like Jesus* (Christlike belonging), *the more I am the me I was made to be* (individual uniqueness).

The elephant in the room that we may need to name before going any further is that identity and salvation are two different conversations. And while they may be related, one doesn't necessarily lead to the other. How we talk about identity, however, may either welcome or deny us the privilege of talking about salvation with one another. So before deciding that identity is a conversation to tackle, I invite you to decide that the people with whom you wish to have that conversation are first meant to be loved.

A KALEIDOSCOPE

Let's return to the definition of the word *identity*: it was, in its origin, synonymous with the word for identical, *idem*, meaning "exactly the same." An idiom still used today is *idem per idem* (Latin for "the same for the same," where no new information is added). In other words, repetition for emphasis. In fact, God employs this idiom (perhaps invents it?) in Exodus 3:14 when God says "I AM WHO I AM." In this turn of phrase, making sameness explicitly clear where no alternative exists, God first declares God's own identity.

Later, in Exodus 33:19, God uses the idiom again, saying, "I will have mercy on whom I will have mercy, and I will have compassion on whom I will have compassion." God doubles down on the truth of who God is in this use of same-for-same language that leaves mercy and compassion in God's hands but leaves no one out in its expression. Ultimately, because God's mercy and compassion are lavished on us according to God's will, we are left with little room to withhold it if we are to bear God's image in Christlikeness, idem per idem. Who we are is because of who Jesus is, and Jesus is what God is like. If we want people to know the great I Am, our mercy and compassion must somehow bear the resemblance of "repetition for emphasis." More mercy. More compassion. Because God will show mercy on whomever God chooses. And we are to do the same.

Idem is similar to the word *ditto*. Fascinatingly, the expression *idem ditto* means "exactly the same." *Idem per idem* and *ditto* are still used today, notably in legal documents. By the late sixteenth century, the word *identity* had evolved from *idem* (meaning "the same") to *identitas*, meaning the quality of being identical. And in our English translations of Scripture, that holds true: our identity as children of God extends from our Christlikeness, our image-bearing nature, a family resemblance so to speak. If we want others to know the mercy and compassion of a God who *is* love, and if we are to make disciples, our identity is meant to be *idem per idem* like Jesus. Or plainly put, Jesus, ditto.

What if we aren't at war with the world's definition of identity? What if we just haven't been clear about ours?

The identity of each one of us is a kaleidoscope of so many variables and defining features: DNA, hopes and dreams, culture, abilities, ethnicity, sex, gender, sexual orientation, and more. The problem for some of us is that we immediately assume that the conversation will only be about gender and sexuality.

But identity isn't any one thing; rather, it is myriad shiny objects meant to catch the Light and reflect beauty to those with eyes to see (Matthew 5:14–16). When we invite kids to point their kaleidoscopes at the light of the world, the tiny pieces of who they are come alive, the colors begin to dance, and wonder is captured and reflects this vibrant image back at us.

We were made to reflect the image of God to those around us through the love of Jesus and by the leading of the Spirit. This is who we are. This is our identity. And the more we look like Jesus in the process, the more we grow to be who we were always made to be. There are big conversations to have about aspects of our identity and how we show up in the world as disciples. Let's make sure that our kids are ready for those moments by first giving them a solid foundation of truth about who, and Whose, they are.

They will want to understand how the kaleidoscope works. But let's start by getting lost in the wonder and beauty of it—by standing in a puddle of the light of the world and knowing who Jesus is first.

IS THERE HOPE IN
THE TENSION?

I have the sense that few are willing to steward a conversation about identity for the sake of the ones it stands to affect with measurable outcomes: the church's emerging generations. This generation of young people is less tolerant to binary thinking, less likely to stay for the sake of tradition, less willing to comply with in/out, us/them religious rhetoric because such frameworks have caged in people groups for centuries, and they know it. Moreover, they will have none of it.

To be clear: Issues of inclusion and, perhaps more significantly, exclusion in the church have existed forever. Patriarchy and misogyny, sexism, racism, bigotry, classism, and ableism (to name a few) have plagued Western Christian culture for centuries. We have justified our rule of law, and in so doing we have not only passively allowed exclusion but aggressively insisted on who's in and who's out for all kinds of reasons that we said were found between the lines of Scripture.

And we have also watched people groups rise up and form their own communities, yes, even their own churches, in order to create safe spaces of belonging—if for no other reason than safety and belonging have not been everyone's experience of the church. This should grieve us. We need to take an honest look at the very real divides and locked doors of our faith communities and question our motives. It's as if we think we have all the goodness, love, joy (you know, all the fruit of the Spirit) inside our buildings and we keep it for ourselves. So tell me: What is the purpose of this fruit? Will it not rot if stored instead of shared?

Further, why do we keep deciding who "our neighbor" (Leviticus 19:18; Mark 12:31) is and what loving them is supposed to look like? In his book reflecting on a Christian response to the Muslim faith, theologian Miroslav Volf writes, "Love properly understood *is* God—the font of all creation and the ultimate goal of all desires; God properly understood *is* love."[1] If Jesus is what God is like, and God is love, and every human ever is an image bearer of Love, why are we excluding anyone from the gospel simply by deciding that what (we think) we see in them (and likely don't understand) disqualifies them from the fruit we are hoarding for ourselves?

And to be fair, we must admit that we have changed our own rules over the years. We have changed our minds before and been wrong. We have changed our minds and are better for it too. The question is: What changes lead to kingdom expansion, radical hospitality, humble worship, and a presence of the living God that is undeniable throughout our communities?

Originally, I imagined this book would be called "Not Disqualified." That's how I believe we are meant to see every image bearer—that is, every person. But if I try to take a posture of grace and mercy as I work to find words that include all people, I realize I must extend the same grace and mercy to those who were raised to believe that some people are simply too sinful, too deviant, too rebellious, or too much. And while holding that tension, I will instead declare that all are *invited* to the table, and no one is disqualified from the grace and mercy of Jesus, a life of love in Jesus' name, and a place in the kingdom of God. Not even the Christians who are working hard to exclude some of God's own beloveds today.

This is the way of Jesus: he started conversations, he sat down in unsacred spaces, he overturned tables in sacred ones, he walked, he wondered, he asked questions, but he never denied someone an invitation to his presence. So this is where we, as Jesus followers, must begin: All are included. Every person is sacred. Every personhood is held together by a DNA strand that is the very image of the Creator of the universe, and all are invited to claim that identity and walk in the fullness of who we were made to be. Just like everyone else.

So why is there such tension in this conversation? Where does it come from? At its worst, it results from a myopic understanding of who can enter the kingdom—namely, those who adhere to a set of rules and social constructs agreed upon by denominations and governing bodies (typically and historically, but not exclusively, groups made up of cisgender, heterosexual white men). For many, the role of the local church evolved into religious gatekeeping, ensuring that those who enter abide by the agreed-upon rules (and reassuring those who follow the rules that they are safe). In short, fear-based theology led to behavior management both inside and outside the walls of the church. For those of us whose lives fit neatly within the prescribed rules, we sometimes think our talk about Jesus is the invitation. But for many, it is the list of clausal inclusions that qualify us to be on one side or the other, according to our human constructs. And much to the surprise of those who are "in," it is equally clear to those who are "out" that they are not welcome inside the gate.

Jesus didn't do this. Jesus did not stand at the temple door and stamp the hands of those who could or could not hang out with him. And you likely don't either. But others know. They know whether they are welcome to be fully present. I know that my fullness is not welcome in a place that denies women the right to use their gifts (because the rule-makers have declared women unsuited to receive certain gifts). A person of color may feel uncomfortable engaging with a primarily white congregation, especially one with historically white practices of worship. A transgender person may assume they are unwelcome because Christians all over the world have been vocal about their disgust and rejection of them.

In fact, during the span of his ministry, Jesus didn't hang out too much at the temple. For the Christians who say things like "*They* [whomever they are] are welcome to come in, but . . ."— don't worry. Those you have already judged aren't expecting to find Jesus inside your walls, because they have not met him at the door. They have experienced your glances, they have heard the messages. They have been told what you think of them. They're not trying to change your mind. They're trying to go to church. And whether it's a lack of a ramp into the building or the way people are dressed or the flag that you fly (or don't fly) or the bathroom facilities, people know whether they're allowed to go to church with you. They know. You can stop whispering under your breath because your building is screaming.

Yet, I have hope for this conversation. I believe we risk nothing when we decide to offer radical hospitality to all people above everything else.

HOSPITALITY

Thanks to a Messianic Jewish mentor, the Jewishness of Jesus has fascinated me for years. To be honest, it fostered in me a hyperactive FOMO (fear of missing out) on what I don't know about why Jesus did certain things, why he talked about certain topics in particular ways, and what he meant by certain phrases rather than what I think he meant based on my own limited, Western, non-Jewish understanding. I had some familiarity with Hanukkah and Shabbat and Passover, but what was I misunderstanding or even just reading past because, culturally, the Christian church has not pursued its full inheritance as co-heirs with Christ?

One of the virtues of Jewish culture that Western Christians may misunderstand most profoundly is that of hospitality. Don't get me wrong, many of us have figured out the potluck, pancake supper, and frozen meals for people experiencing a challenging season. But in Jewish practice, hospitality is more than social, more than food, more than an invitation:

> One of the virtues for which one enjoys the fruits in this world and obtains the principal reward in the world to come, hospitality, is, according to [Rabbi] Johanan, even more important than prayer or, according to [Rabbi] Judah, than receiving the divine presence.[2]

> In the pre-modern world, without ubiquitous hotels and rapid transportation, wayfarers were often dependent on those whom they encountered en route. Jewish communities traditionally provided for Jews passing through their locales, whether they were indigent or simply in transit. The Talmud even says that welcoming guests is "greater than welcoming the Divine Presence [*Shekhinah*]."[3]

Given that Jesus was raised to know and live with this understanding of hospitality, how does that begin to inform and reveal the limited expressions of hospitality in the modern church? If hospitality could be considered more important than prayer, and welcoming guests is greater than welcoming the presence of God, consider the lack of welcome that Jesus experienced throughout his ministry. Consider his invitation to dust off your sandals and go. Consider the experience of Jesus' birth for Mary and Joseph as they were met with no welcome anywhere.

Reimagine, then, the warning of Mark 6:4–6: "Jesus said to them, 'A prophet is not without honor except in his own town, among his relatives and in his own home.' He could not do any miracles there, except lay his hands on a few sick people and heal them. He was amazed at their lack of faith." For the Jewish people, faith and hospitality are spiritually intertwined. I imagine that Jesus was making this statement out of his own experience. The lack of hospitality he was shown was directly proportionate to the lack of faith, or prayer, of the people. And that lack of faith lacked an expectancy of God's presence, perhaps even a craving for it. God, let us not expect a miracle where we have not first welcomed your divine presence.

And then there's Matthew 10:14–15: "If anyone will not welcome you or listen to your words, leave that home or town and shake the dust off your feet. Truly I tell you, it will be more bearable for Sodom and Gomorrah on the day of judgment than for that town." I always imagined Jesus clapping his hands together and wiping them on his tunic as he spoke this, with an air of disdain hanging in the balance. His is a bold statement. But if you consider welcoming guests to be the greatest good, the gravity of his words settles like the dust left on the disciples' feet. This isn't the turn-and-storm-out moment that I imagined. This is a your-feet-are-still-dirty moment, which implies that the divine presence is not present. If your feet are still dirty, you have not been welcomed. Your feet have not been washed. You have not been shown hospitality, so do not stay where God is not present.

Is it worth the risk to welcome guests so that the Holy Spirit's presence would be undeniably experienced, creating a radically invitational altar where all are able to come to Jesus freely, just as they are, fully present, fully known by their Creator? What would such hospitality look like? I think Paul had an idea: "I pray that you, being rooted and established in love, may have power, together with all the Lord's holy people, to grasp how wide and long and high and deep is the love of Christ, and to know this love that surpasses knowledge—that you may be filled to the measure of all the fullness of God" (Ephesians 3:17–19).

This is my hope in the tension; that being rooted in love and grafted to the vine (John 15:1) would lead us to extend our branches and love one another with the wide, long, high, deep love of Christ that is greater than knowledge or understanding:

> Just as you received Christ Jesus as Lord, continue to live your lives in him, rooted and built up in him, strengthened in the faith as you were taught, and overflowing with thankfulness.
>
> See to it that no one takes you captive through hollow and deceptive philosophy, which depends on human tradition and the elemental spiritual forces of this world rather than on Christ. (Colossians 2:6–8)

Knowledge of the law, through theology or a denominational confession of faith, is the deep work of those who have gone before us and is meant to help point us to God and to help us better understand Scripture. It is the work of the church to keep from allowing any of the good work of God's beloved thinkers and dreamers and writers to become "deceptive philosophy." The love of Christ is greater, and this love alone fills us to the measure. If our philosophies depend on human tradition and not on Jesus, we betray this love. By this love we know God and are known (John 13:35). And because of this love, hope is a strong and trustworthy anchor (Hebrews 6:19).

8

WHERE DO YOU FEEL
THE TENSION?

We know that tension can arise from our faith traditions, deeply held beliefs, and theology. We have different denominations for many reasons. So it isn't surprising that tension is often felt in what are often the first questions in this conversation: How do you define identity? Who am I? What is identity?

Do you know how many times kids will google the questions they're wondering about or afraid to ask? All of them. All the times. So I googled "definition of identity" because I wanted to know what they would see first. Here's what came up:

- The condition or fact of being the same or exactly alike; sameness; oneness.
- An equation which is true for all values of the variables which appear in it. Example: $x^2 - y^2 = (x + y)(x - y)$.
- Information, such as an identification number, used to establish or prove a person's individuality, as in providing access to a credit account.

- The definition of identity is who you are, the way you think about yourself, the way you are viewed by the world, and the characteristics that define you.
- A sameness between two items or designs such that one violates patent rights held by the other.
- The sameness some individuals share to make up the same kind or universal.
- The difference or character that marks off an individual from the rest of the same kind, selfhood.
- A name or persona—the mask or appearance one presents to the world—by which one is known.
- Knowledge of who one is.

It's important to acknowledge that in printed English-language texts, the use of the word *identity* was relatively insignificant until about forty years ago. Other words that have followed a similar use-case curve include *gender*, *sexuality*, and *spirituality*. (Conversely, the word *soul* has followed a rather jagged, equal opposite curve, though it seems to take

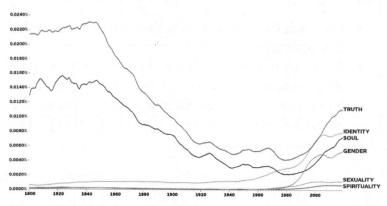

Appearance of the words *identity, spirituality, soul, gender, sexuality,* and *truth* in printed texts, 1800 through 2019. Google Books Ngram Viewer, http://books.google.com/ngrams.

the same path as *truth*, beginning to rise in the last couple of decades as well.) Now, imagine being a child living in the tension of these words, these definitions, these conflicting ideas of "who I am."

James D. Fearon, a professor of political science at Stanford University, says,

> Despite this vastly increased and broad-ranging interest in "identity," the concept itself remains something of an enigma. . . . "Identity" in its present incarnation has a double sense. It refers at the same time to social categories and to the sources of an individual's self-respect or dignity. There is no necessary linkage between these things. In ordinary language, at least, one can use "identity" to refer to personal characteristics or attributes that cannot naturally be expressed in terms of a social category, and in some contexts certain categories can be described as "identities" even though no one sees them as central to their personal identity.[1]

According to Dictionary.com, the first two meanings of identity are

> 1. the state or fact of remaining the same one or ones, as under varying aspects or conditions
> 2. the condition of being oneself or itself, and not another[2]

You may recall from our earlier discussion of the etymology of *identity* that the word began as *idem* in Latin, meaning "same." In late Latin, the word became *identitas*, with the same meaning. In sixteenth-century English, *identity* came into use with the full definition "quality of being identical." Yet when we look at the similes and synonyms listed in any modern thesaurus, we find this list: individuality, self, selfhood, ego, personality, character, originality, distinctiveness, distinction, singularity, peculiarity, uniqueness.

Not one of those words means "the same" or "the quality of being identical." Somewhere along the way, the word's original meaning and definition became the antithesis of what we now mean when we use it. It's not a problem in and of itself unless you are trying to navigate a conversation about identity today and believe it to mean exclusively one or the other. And sometimes we do use the word that way, affixing it to a particular aspect of an individual or an identifier of belonging. Sometimes we use it to declare who we are exclusively, rather than also being known by those with whom we spend time, the hobbies and habits we choose, and our preferences. As Christians, we remember, we do or ought to have aspects of our identity rooted in a kind of sameness—we are to be known by our Christlike love, as in John 13:35: "This is how everyone will know that you are my disciples" (CEB).

Imagine being a child of any age today and living in this tension. I know you feel that tension, too, and the confusion it can cause. I was raised with the adage "The devil is the author of confusion," and why wouldn't the enemy come for the very core beliefs about identity, how our kids see themselves, and how we talk about who they were made to be? He comes "only to steal and kill and destroy; I [Jesus] have come that they may have life, and have it to the full" (John 10:10). At best, our kids are confused by what we say in the church and what they experience in the world; at worst, they are being destroyed because of the tension we are leaving them to navigate alone. We need high spiritual ambition for today's kids. Set the spiritual bar high and remove any hindrance (Hebrews 12:1) that would keep them from jumping. They are welcome to full access to the Holy Spirit and relationship with Jesus just as they are. Our goal is to build a straight, debris-free track that invites them to run hard and jump right into the Father's arms.

I was holding my second child, rocking back and forth while standing at the back of a church service one Sunday listening to a guest speaker. He was a passionate speaker with a convicting message that was birthed in the prison system after living for years as North America's most wanted man (yep, he was number one on that list). While he was filled with grace and mercy in this moment, you could see the scars of a former life all over him, and he was unwilling to allow even one breath to be wasted sharing anything other than the good news of a good God who means it when he says that he loves you and his love is for "the least of these."

As this man's rich bass tones resonated through the room, he took a moment to address the heaviness that some were likely feeling because of his story. And he met that conviction with a sobering warning: "Brothers and sisters, if you think the enemy is coming for you, you're wrong. He already knows by your life, your walk, and your talk if you are available to him or not. He's not coming for you. He's coming for your kids."

My three-week-old sleeping son startled as I gasped and began to weep. The speaker went on to talk about how it worked in his former world and how his gang would prey on children at playgrounds, in parks, in your neighborhood. But let's be clear about what he wasn't saying: he was not saying "Do not let your kids play outside." He was saying "We have an enemy."

In the same way, and in the words of a dear friend (who was quoting a dear friend), "Don't hear what I'm not saying." I am not saying there is one way to define identity and to shut down others. I am not saying to keep your kids from exploring their identity. I am not saying we shouldn't be asking all kinds of questions and laying them out before our Father like Hezekiah laying out the letters of Sennacherib before battle in 2 Kings 19.

What I am saying is that the world is a battlefield—we are raising kids in the middle of it, and we *get to* walk alongside them, even when it doesn't make sense to us. Even when we are confused. Even when they are confused. Even when we don't have the answers. Even if it means we disagree. And on this battlefield, we serve the one true King who is already victorious, and we do not turn to the right or to the left. We stand firm on what we are called to: a hope that has a name and that holds the tension for us when we are stretched to the full.

The only way I have been able to reconcile this tension is in the person of Jesus, our living hope. And the more I look like Jesus (sameness), the more I get to become who I was made to be (uniqueness). And the more I am like him, the more likely I am to see him in others.

CAN WE RESOLVE THE TENSION?

This polarity of individual uniqueness versus a sense of belonging is not generally experienced as a tension for today's emergent generations. It is the ubiquitous and yet ever-evolving ideology of authenticity: I get to say who I am, and you get to believe me. It might change next week, but both are authentic to the moment, and you get to accept that. My uniqueness is my highest value and most invaluable contribution. *But I also want to belong.* Loneliness is very real for today's kids and is at the heart of today's mental health crisis (just google "loneliness epidemic").

According to Victoria Bennett, founder and CEO of a social and academic educational services company, "Gen Alpha, or those born after 2010, have grown up in a digital world, but that hasn't stopped them from feeling lonely. In a recent survey, over half of Gen Alpha respondents said they feel lonely at least once a week." Bennett suggests the following as some of the ways that social groups—whether friend groups, clubs of common interest, or groups that share identity markers—can help combat loneliness:

- Provide a safe, welcoming environment where young people can connect with others who share their interests.
- Encourage participants to share their thoughts and feelings, fostering a sense of community and empathy.
- Facilitate social skills development through group activities and games.
- Encourage participants to practice empathy and emotional intelligence through group discussions.
- Offer opportunities for building connections within the group, which can boost self-esteem and provide a sense of purpose.[1]

Beneath this seemingly shape-shifting presentation of authenticity, what kids want most is to be accepted for who they are and where they are on their journey today, not just aspirationally for what we hope they will become or pray they'll outgrow. And they want people to do life with who don't need them to change, even though they will. They just want to be welcome. They also want to know that when they change or even just change their minds, we will still love them, believe them, invite them, allow them to continue to learn and grow and become.

All of us have to be permitted to change our minds. We have to be allowed to not know *yet*, to not have all the answers, to be confused, to wonder, to try, and to try again. This is part of the process of learning, growing, and becoming. *All of it* can be authentic, even if it means I see myself differently over time. Goodness, I hope I have changed over time! I hope I've softened my gaze, become less rigid in my thinking, asked more questions than had answers, and lived with more holy than lurid curiosity for how others grow and change, too. Especially if I believe that I get to be more the me I was made to be as I become more like Jesus. This is, after all, the essence of discipleship.

When we walk alongside kids as they explore who they are today, we have to know two things for sure: what is true about them no matter what, and that they will change over time. Allowing for something to be true "today" or "sometimes" not only permits a growth mindset, but also leaves room for the possibility of uncertainty, experimenting, and seasons in life. It also leaves room for the invitation to change your mind about what you thought you knew because of what you are learning as you grow, too.

When one of my daughters was twelve, I asked her whether she thought she wanted to be a mother, and her answer was an unequivocal, unhesitant no. When I asked her why not, she simply replied, "Because I am twelve." If, one day, she holds a child of her own in her arms, I don't think I'll look back at that moment and say, "I didn't see this coming!" But it's true for her today. And it might be true later. But it doesn't have to be, and that really matters. This is different from what is true about her no matter what. And the only things that are always true about her are the things God has declared over her: she is known, loved, included, made in God's own image, a co-heir with Jesus, a treasure, a blessing, all that, yes! And she is also a person to whom God has given choice and agency. And the truth is, she can find her way through all life's maybes by following the way, the truth, the life: Jesus.

For racialized kids, the color of their skin is part of their origin story, and it will be true of them always. But the abuse, exclusion, and injustice that comes because of it doesn't have to be. (We, especially white people, have work to do, friends.) Some truths are hard. But because we have a hope that does not drop the rope on us, we need to take advantage of the do-overs afforded us by the grace of God. Ending the abuse and moving toward inclusion and justice does not simply look like the opposite of what occurred in the past. Equity for racialized kids starts with noticing, with moving toward them, with sitting down and learning from them. A seat at the table is not equity. Asking whether they'd like to join you (and if not, why not), what they'd like to eat, and if they'd like to help set the menu and the table is a start.

What has been true for kids who identify differently from the majority is the result of truths that should never have been punitive. Jesus said, "Let the little children come to me, and do not hinder them, for the kingdom of God belongs to such as these. Truly I tell you, anyone who will not receive the kingdom of God like a little child will never enter it" (Luke 18:16–17). Get down on their level. They know the way.

Centering on Jesus has the power to shift our discomfort with the tension. In his book *Centered-Set Church*, Mark Baker talks about what it looks like to be a "centered set" faith community, naming how this approach contrasts from being a "bounded set" or "fuzzy set" community.[2]

Bounded-set faith community: An obvious, static fence line, so to speak, distinguishes Christians from non-Christians, or "true" Christians from "lukewarm" Christians. The fence is usually made up of a list of correct beliefs and certain visible behaviors that those who are

Bounded set

"in" can see and measure and will evaluate. A bounded-set church tends toward a sense of hierarchy and judgmentalism. It hinders transparency, accountability, and humility. It allows those who do not conform to be shamed, rebuked, and even publicly exposed.

Fuzzy-set faith community: In response to the problematic (and often abusive) line-drawing of the bounded-set approach, a fuzzy church erases the line. The grounds for distinction and judgmentalism are gone, and a "you do you" ethos is adopted. The fuzziness, however, erodes the

Fuzzy set

group's identity and even sense of belonging. What makes us "us"? A fuzzy approach lacks a sense of call to a different way of living (a Christlikeness as laid out in Scripture) and inhibits loving others fully because of a lack of intimacy and resulting accountability or mutuality. A fuzzy-set church tends toward blandness. And in my experience, the life of discipleship is anything but bland (and is not meant to be). Like the smeared marks of an eraser, the fuzziness reminds people that there was once something that set them apart but leaves no sense of unity other than "we are not bounded-set." This approach is disorienting, and there is little compelling or spiritually motivating about it.

Centered-set faith community: A centered-set approach discerns who belongs to the group by observing people's relationship with the center—Jesus Christ. The group includes all those who are oriented toward the center, the well, the source of living water. Their common direction brings

Centered set

unity. There is space to struggle or step back because everyone recognizes that they are all in process—moving closer to the center in their journey with Jesus. (Those facing away from the center may once have been part of the group but are oriented away from the center. Ultimately, what distinguishes those in the group from those outside the group is not specific characteristics but the direction they are facing or moving—closer to the center if even on an indirect path.) A centered approach remedies the problems of a bounded church that motivate a fuzzy church to blur the boundaries while also avoiding the confusion or even apathy of a fuzzy approach. There is room for disagreement while maintaining unity. There is room for the Holy Spirit to speak and reorient the flock. There is room to arrive at different conclusions about ancient texts while still holding one's orientation toward Jesus, rather than toward rules (or lack thereof).

As we endeavor to cut through confusion with truth, we can look to Scripture to lead us well in this conversation. Beyond our bodies, who does Jesus say we are? How does God name us? What are we called to by the power of the Holy Spirit? Where would you turn in your Bible to find unwavering truth about who you are? Here are a few passages to get you started: Psalm 139; John 15:9–17; Zephaniah 3:17–20; Romans 15:1–7. Take a moment to read a passage, or remind yourself of a favorite if you already have one.

Knowing who God says we are empowers us to name the truths with those we love and do life with while sitting in the tension of what we don't yet know. It sounds like saying, "I don't know that I have the answer to your really brave question, but I do know this . . . You are loved, you are known and adored for who you are, even if you don't understand, even if you're scared, even when you can't see where Jesus is leading, even when you feel alone." It also sounds like, "Thank you for being brave enough to ask tough questions, to say hard things out loud, to wonder and want for more. And thank you for inviting me to sit with you in those questions. Thank you for trusting me."

When someone has the courage to come to you with a question about their identity—their purpose, their value—know that they are saying a few things between the lines of what is being voiced. First, they feel safe enough to trust you with their questions, which tells you that you have loved them well. Keep loving well even in the messy middle. And second, staying present in the moment matters more than having the answers. They chose you. Honor their choice and be still.

In that moment when the tension between knowing and not knowing what to say is most felt, you can lean on a few truths about the Bible:

1. Not all answers about identity can be found in Scripture. It is a love letter, not a textbook. What is true about who God says I am is found in Scripture. But these aren't the only questions today's kids are asking. Saying "I don't know" or "That's a really hard question" or "It seems so confusing" are beautiful answers when they are the right answers. A beautiful source of reassurance can be found in Psalm 139: while I don't know what plans God has for me or how I'm made to fit into the world around me, I do know that God has had that plan since before I lived even one day. Knowing that God knows can be very comforting.

2. Every answer about being known, loved, seen, designed, and led by the Creator *can* be found in Scripture. Scripture is sufficient to define, shape, and lead any conversation about identity. We can start with Scripture as we share the pencil sketches of God's magnificent creativity with one another. This idea of being seen by God was first articulated by Hagar, who ran away after being mistreated by Sarai, Abram's wife. God

spoke to Hagar in the wilderness, and she replied 'You are the God who sees me,' for she said, 'I have now seen the One who sees me' (Genesis 16:13). Later, in Exodus 3, Moses meets God at the burning bush, and God tells Moses that he has seen the suffering of his children, he has heard their complaints, and his heart has been moved to compassion and he will come to save them. From the first stories in the Bible through the end of its last book, we meet a God who sees, knows, and cares. That is who God is. And that deserves to be at the center of the conversation.

3. Who I am is found in who Jesus is, first. If I want to know who I was made to be, I have to know who Jesus is to me. If a person does not yet have a relationship with Jesus, this takes priority over any other conversation—not necessarily by talking about Jesus, but by *being* Jesus to someone who has invited you to draw near. Let them experience him in order to grow curious about him. Jesus said "Follow me" no less than seventeen times in the Gospels. And he did not say it to those who already understood what that meant. He said it to a couple of anglers, a tax collector, those who were willing to give up who they said they were for who Jesus said he was. Perhaps the best examples of this identity exchange are in Matthew and John: "'Come, follow me,' Jesus said, 'and I will send you out to fish for people.' At once they left their nets and followed him" (Matthew 4:19–20). Jesus said, "I am the light of the world. Whoever follows me will never walk in darkness, but will have the light of life" (John 8:12). Draw others into the light. Love them in the pool of light that you cast because you know Jesus. The rest of the identity conversation is enlightened and informed by how we choose to center on Jesus and, therefore, how we center on the ones he centers on: the one in front of you.

4. The values used to define me are set by the One who created me in God's own image. My identity is found in my image-bearing status *and* in how I was knit together to bear that image. There are core contributors to a person's identity: culture, physical attributes, spirituality, socioeconomic status, ability, ethnicity, gender, sexuality (just to name a few), and they matter. Who I am is found not only in who God made me to be, but also in how I am made to be like Jesus in the body that God wired to show up in the world as me. My character, nature, body, mind, and spirit were created soft and pliable, made to be shaped in Christlikeness: who I am versus who I am becoming. "For we are God's handiwork, created in Christ Jesus to do good works, which God prepared in advance for us to do" (Ephesians 2:10). If we don't start with Jesus, we end up disqualifying people from the gospel who don't yet know him. We make decisions about what we see, where they are from, and how they show up, and thereby create division instead of invitation. But we are called to unity, which means we need to model unity.

This is how we resolve the tensions: Start with Jesus. Walk with Jesus. Be like Jesus. Let your identity be shaped by Jesus. And invite others to do the same by deciding who *you* are in him, first.

10

WHERE DO WE GO FROM HERE?

Let's return to the story in Ezra, to the forgetful people who grieved and celebrated simultaneously but who also found their identity rooted in remembrance. This is one of those stories in Scripture where I am reminded that we have been here before: in the tension of the way things are, and with God's promise to make all things new (Isaiah 43:19; Revelation 21:5). God's family has had more than one "it's not supposed to be this way" moment before. Certain cultural moments, shifts in theology, or even our collective understanding of, or agreement with, particular theological constructs have left us wondering if God is with us. Those who were there at the establishment of the first temple were expecting fire from heaven at the second. That fire didn't come, yet God was near. We see God's fingerprints all over the story as Israel remembers, and we can see our own fingerprints all over what comes next: They forget. Again.

It's okay to sit in the rubble of what may feel like a fallen temple and ask God, "What now?" God is not surprised by our confusion. Jesus is not disappointed by your dismay. The

Holy Spirit is not afraid of your questions. They've heard them before. We have been here before, family. Our job is to remember: remember that God is who God says God is, and we are who God says we are.

That moment of remembrance was always going to require more than a morning of worship or seven days of sweets like we read in Nehemiah 8 about Israel's celebration that followed. Remembering who we are requires reminders along the way and in community. It requires habits of storytelling, gathering, and celebrating or lamenting (or both at the same time), which create memories. Without these habits, remembering is a ritual; with these habits, remembering builds relationships.

I am sure that those who remembered that week of delicious food and celebration would have told their children and their children's children. But you can't taste it on your tongue if you weren't there. You don't smell all the goodness or hear the sounds of laughter ring in your ear if you only hear a story about it. If I had only ever read about mango, I would not love it as much as I do. If I had tasted it only once, years ago, from a grocery store, not only would I not talk about it, but I likely would not remember it as anything special. I'm not sure I would even notice it, let alone pick it up every time I'm in the produce section and smell it. It would be "that one time I was in Chinatown" and not "my favorite food ever, you *have* to try it."

I can read about mango, look at pictures, and listen to other people who also enjoy talking about it. I can even look up recipes with mango in it, prepare it for people I love, and watch them enjoy it. We can even talk about what might have made the recipe better, why we like it or don't like it, and whether it belongs in a certain recipe.

Do you see what I'm getting at?

It doesn't matter what those around you, in your social media feed or in your community, *think* about mango. I'm asking you: What do you *love* about mango? Do you remember the first time you tasted it? Maybe you've never had a perfectly ripe Ataulfo mango. Let me tell you about my first bite . . . It is with this same passion, anticipation, and delight that we are meant to share the good news of Jesus. So if the gospel gets the first word in a conversation about identity, you have to love it—like *really* love it.

So what does this look like? Where does one begin? Here are practical steps you can take to move you from "What now?" to "Let's try, together":

1. Decide that this conversation is about relationship. You can read all about your perfect match, but until you spend time with that person, you're not in a relationship.

    a. Go back to the foundation: Build your relationship with Scripture and decide in advance the role it will play in the conversation. What do you expect Scripture to do to support you and the kids you're talking to? What is its purpose in your life? How will you share what you know about the Bible? The hope you have for this conversation comes from first reading and then sharing the glorious story of God's heart to partner with us throughout history.

    b. You can read about plumbing, but it doesn't make you a plumber. What does it look like in your life to take what you read in the pages of Scripture and live it out? Talk about how it's more than an ancient text to you, and share how you know that to be true. What have you seen? What have you heard? How have you experienced the presence of the living God through the living and active Word of God? I was recently reminded that the primary point of a God-breathed scripture is to be useful: "All Scripture is God-breathed and is useful for teaching, rebuking, correcting and training in righteousness, so that the servant of God may be thoroughly equipped for every good work" (2 Timothy 3:16–17). These active verbs are possible only in relationship. And don't ignore the "so that." *So that the servant of God may be thoroughly equipped.* That's you. That's me. That's everyone with whom we are invited to walk this out. That's what makes it living and active. If this is the primary purpose of Scripture, then its very useful nature requires relationship. Discipleship is relationship. Be a disciple in order to disciple (*idem per idem*).

c. If I devour Scripture the way I devour mango, it will either make me look good (she's so devoted, learned, knowledgeable) or make Jesus look good (she really loves him). The first runs the risk of saying "Look at me." The other says "Look at him." Create a habit of Scripture if you don't yet have a relationship with it. And do it until it makes you rise to your feet, fall on your face, weep and laugh. Be the one that remembers. Be the generation who celebrates. Be the remnant in this scattered kingdom.

2. Intimacy with the Holy Spirit is something that satisfies the experience of exile. If you are tired, hungry, or thirsty, she can satisfy.

    a. I don't think it was the physical book of the law that caused such a fuss in the story of Ezra and Nehemiah. I think Israel was reminded of the intimacy they once knew with a loving God who made a way for them to enter his presence, and that some had known, and the people immediately felt both satisfied and hungry for more at the same time.

    b. Regardless of how you feel about the cultural moment and the conversation we are navigating within it, what today's kids are facing, or how a conversation about identity seems to foster confusion over curiosity, we are not in exile. We do not need to conclude that our kids are lost or that the church has been reduced to rubble. The church might not be the way it used to be or the way you remember it if you attended Sunday school as a child, but the church's evolution is not necessarily its greatest issue. Doubling down on some of the bounded-set fences and rigid rites of passage may be more dangerous than a flexibility in this conversation. The church is God's plan A for God's family until Jesus returns. There is no plan B. And there is no ground on this globe that is not fertile. Think mustard seed (Matthew 13:31–33).

    c. Further, we need to decide to go *with* our kids. While this isn't exile, we would not send them into Babylon and say, "Best of luck! I'm here if you need me!" Choose to stay present enough to be available in any moment. Present enough to hold space and time for their thoughts and questions. Present enough to know when to rescue and when to rest. Present enough to remind them, to remember together, to eat sweets.

d. The concept of "mutual submission" is well documented in Ephesians 5 and 1 Peter 2 and 5. Intimacy for such a tender conversation requires mutuality, and mutuality, by definition, requires vulnerability and intimacy. Note that according to Paul and Peter, it isn't just younger people submitting to their elders; they say *submit yourselves*. The humility this conversation requires will also require some practice.

3. Develop an insatiable appetite for Scripture. Once you've tasted and seen that it is good, you begin to crave more of what it has to feed you. And how you talk about the Bible, its purpose, and the role it plays in your life will shape the way you share it with others.

a. While Jesus promises an abundant life, I'm not sure he meant for us to conflate his words with prosperity, money, or stuff. This is what I mean about an appetite for Scripture: the more you read it, the more you measure what you may have been taught or understand against what Scripture actually says. I think the Western church is guilty of amassing wealth and hoarding it for our own in part because we've adopted the world's scarcity framework as an example. Somehow, we have come to believe that there isn't enough for everyone. When we talk about scarcity, however, we often define its opposite as "lavish abundance." There isn't enough of that for everyone (food scarcity, malnutrition, and displaced people are real crises), but we know there is absolutely enough Jesus for everyone. So, what if our understanding of abundance is flawed, and the opposite of scarcity in the kingdom looks more like sufficiency? It is the difference between enoughness versus lavishness: When the apostle Paul talks about abundant blessing, he talks about needs being met: "God is able to bless you abundantly, so that in all things at all times, having all that you need, you will abound in every good work" (2 Corinthians 9:8). Our role in making disciples is also to ensure that others have enough. And we do not get to choose who deserves enough. You cannot earn God's grace. It's freely available. Whom do you need to extend it to so that they have enough to engage with you in this conversation?

b. What if the abundant life is one where everyone has what they need? God promised to meet our needs. There's that word again. So what do we truly need from God that only God can provide? I promise you, the answer to that question is a lavish and abundant life full in the fullness of God, and there is plenty for each one of us. God does not withhold love from those who seek him. "But seek first his kingdom and his righteousness, and all these things will be given to you as well," Jesus says (Matthew 6:33). Making sure kids have what they need *so that* they can participate fully in this conversation is essential.

Are you hungry for more? Do you long to see the kingdom of God expanded in real time? Do you crave a glimpse of
heaven on earth? Lengthen your table, grab some chairs, and
peel a few more mangoes. There is plenty for everyone, so send
out the invitations. All are welcome to feast on the gospel. I
think it's time to worry more about feeding people than about
whether they know how to hold their fork a certain way.

11

DO MANGOES GROW IN SAMARIA?

Because of our ability to have a relationship with Jesus today by the Holy Spirit, I think it's easy to forget that Jesus lived in a time and place and had an identity as a thirtysomething Jewish man during his years of ministry. Just as your identity—gender, ethnicity, sexuality, abilities, personality, beliefs, and so on—affects how you show up in your world, Jesus also faced expectations to behave a certain way and show up in his identity not as Messiah or Son of God but as Mary's son, that guy from Nazareth.

But Jesus knew who he was beyond what those he did life with understood. And Jesus chose to do things his own way so that one day we would know how to do things his way. What would have changed if Jesus had followed the ways of the temple alone instead of *being* the new Way, with a new covenant? Where is the good news in a good guy who does good things just like everyone else? The point was that he did things the way his Father ordered, and he obeyed in the Spirit. And the world shifted on its axis.

We see this clearly when Jesus visits the woman at the well in John 4. In this story, we find Jesus in Samaria, talking to a woman who was considered an outcast of society. A few radical things are happening here: For starters, Samaria was not a place for proper Jews. Being in "unclean" places meant you were now ceremonially unclean for temple (not enough of a deterrent for Jesus, but worth noting). Whether traveling from Judea to Galilee or the other direction, the fear of encountering a Samaritan was enough reason to take the long way around. Samaria was not a place for those who wished to remain ceremonially clean and thus able to enter the temple.[1] Samaria was where *those* people lived. If Samaritans were characters in the Harry Potter series, they would be mudbloods. And the woman at the well was a Samaritan.

This was more than disdain for a people group; it was absolute segregation based on fear and a result of the exile that led up to the Ezra story. Among the remnant that returned, Samaritans, *identifying with* Judeans, showed up to help rebuild the temple. It was then that the rejection of the Jews from Samaria was galvanized in the culture because of their questionable Jewish descent (they had intermarried over the course of seventy years of exile, which isn't surprising). Centuries of hostility began, and the Samaritans eventually had to build their own temple, unwelcome to worship in Jerusalem.[2]

Despite Samaria's checkered history and the Jews' general dislike of the people of the region, Jesus himself evangelized the area and mandated that the gospel be preached there after his ascension. God's message of salvation extends to all. Ironically, when Jesus first commissioned the twelve disciples, he told them not to enter any town of the Samaritans (Matthew 10). He knew the cost of passing through Samaria. He knew what would happen to their ministries if they mixed with the wrong people. He knew who the disciples were and who they were not, and they weren't *him*. They didn't know what he knew, and they were not there to count the cost; he was.

The divide between Jews and Samaritans was generations old. It was also learned. The Jews and Samaritans hated each other, and when the Jews returned to Israel, they refused to allow the Samaritans to join them in their worship. The Samaritans created their worship system centered on Mount Gerizim and built their own temple not out of rebellion but rather out of a longing to worship with no welcome to do so. (Does this remind you of anything you are seeing in the modern church?)

The Jews thought of the Samaritans as descendants of spiritually corrupt Israelites of the Northern Kingdom, which was made worse by the fact that they had also intermingled with other foreigners who worshiped other gods, regardless of their longing to worship God. They were rejected for *who they were*: Samaritan.

Enter Jesus, stage left, hundreds of years later. In the gospel of John, chapter 4, we read about the conversation between Jesus and the Samaritan woman. Verse 9 confirms that Jews should never have anything to do with Samaritans (let alone a man sit with a woman of her status). Later, in verses 19–23, Jesus acknowledges the rift between the Samaritans and Jews but explains that, in the future, no matter whether someone is a Samaritan or a Jew (or me or you), one can worship God in spirit and truth.[3]

So it's clear that Jesus *shouldn't* be in Samaria, but let's set the stage for his interaction with the woman at the well. Jesus *is* in Samaria, and so is Jacob's well. How beautiful that Jesus, as the life source of "living water," is sitting at the life source of fresh water built by Israel's namesake. Here, Jesus asks the woman for a drink. They both know this is unconventional (to say the least). Their discourse is elegant, poetic, and kind. Jesus doesn't get tripped up on why the woman is there at noon (unusual and impractical) or that she has had many husbands (likely because of her being bought, sold, and discarded). While the former is a result of the latter, the bottom line is that Jesus is talking to a woman who has been rejected by society not only for what are considered her sins, but also for the markers of her identity.

We do this. We reject people for what we think are their sins. *Jesus doesn't.* Jesus sits down and has a conversation. He asks questions, he offers the woman what that well cannot, and he lets her in on a secret: the Father is looking for worshipers in spirit and truth, and she is welcome to be one of them. And she leans in and asks a question back: "Could this be the Messiah?" (v. 29). He arrived at a well with no way of retrieving water, knowing full well that's not why he was there. He was there to welcome one who had never been welcomed before. This is the way of Jesus.

Jesus did not ask her to sort herself out before he sat down. He didn't ask if someone else was available to get him a drink. He did not test her on her worthiness of his presence, let alone the secret of salvation. He saw her for who she was, not who she had become amid a complicated and judged life as a Samaritan woman.

There are people in our world whom we consider to be Samaritans. We might not like to admit it, but we step around them, have opinions about them, and even judge them. Yet our invitation to be loved by Jesus includes his invitation to sit at the well *with, among, beside* the ones who would not otherwise have access to living water.

In Luke 10, just before he tells the parable of the good Samaritan, Jesus finds himself questioned by another expert in the Jewish law. It is clear from the passage that this person was testing Jesus: "Teacher," he asked, "what must I do to inherit eternal life?" (v. 25) Now, we need to understand that this lawyer did not recognize Jesus as Messiah, and as many were in the habit of doing, the expert was goading Jesus' knowledge of Torah to figure him out (read: trip him up). The conversation continues:

> "What is written in the Law?" [Jesus] replied. "How do you read it?"
>
> [The expert] answered, "'Love the Lord your God with all your heart and with all your soul and with all your strength and with all your mind'; and, 'Love your neighbor as yourself.'"
>
> "You have answered correctly," Jesus replied. "Do this and you will live."
>
> But he wanted to justify himself, so he asked Jesus, "And who is my neighbor?" (Luke 10:26–29)

Allow me to interrupt this drama to confess that I, too, have asked this question. Perhaps not out loud (or maybe out loud, you know, in the moments when you double check whether you're being a jerk by not inviting *that* person), but I have definitely wondered whom I *have* to include in this phrase, or perhaps more significantly, whom I can exclude (without moral consequence, of course). Whom do I get a pass on loving? When am I off the hook? Who is my neighbor *so that I can know who isn't*? Loving all people is messy, difficult, frustrating, painful, and costly. I wonder if this lawyer had certain people in mind as he asked this question. More specifically, I wonder if he definitely didn't think the Samaritan was his neighbor.

Jesus knew what he was asking. So, as he often did, he baked the skin of the question right into the dish with a story:

> "A man was going down from Jerusalem to Jericho, when he was attacked by robbers. They stripped him of his clothes, beat him and went away, leaving him half dead. A priest happened to be going down the same road, and when he saw the man, he passed by on the other side. So too, a Levite, when he came to the place and saw him, passed by on the other side. But a Samaritan, as he traveled, came where the man was; and when he saw him, he took pity on him. He went to him and bandaged his wounds, pouring on oil and wine. Then he put the man on his own donkey, brought him to an inn and took care of him. The next day he took out two denarii and gave them to the innkeeper. 'Look after him,' he said, 'and when I return, I will reimburse you for any extra expense you may have.'
>
> "Which of these three do you think was a neighbor to the man who fell into the hands of robbers?"
>
> The expert in the law replied, "The one who had mercy on him."
>
> Jesus told him, "Go and do likewise." (Luke 10:30–37)

We don't know the ethnicity or origin of the man who was beaten and left for dead. This is a spicy detail to leave out. It's easier to focus on how uncomfortable it is that the one whom we are supposed to "go and do likewise" is a Samaritan. But we also step around people simply because they're dirty, they're in a ditch, they did (or didn't) do something to end up there, or they're just different. Everybody wants to be the good Samaritan in this story, but the kicker is that the one who was judged just because of who he was didn't evaluate the person he served before helping him.

We love the story of the good Samaritan, but we wouldn't want to *be* a Samaritan. Notice what Jesus does: he hangs out with one (a woman!), and then he makes another the hero of a story and catches a religious Jewish lawyer in a conundrum: How can the place we are not meant to go and the people we are not meant to mix with produce evidence of *the way* we are meant *to be*?

I am convinced that the religious leaders of the day would not have assumed that Samaritans could have true relationships with God, if for no other reason than they thought Samaritans were unfit for the temple, unclean, and therefore unable to enter God's presence. I am also convinced that we assume that people we see as Samaritans today don't have a relationship with God. Sometimes we assume that someone needs Jesus just because we can't figure out how they can be who they say they are *and* be a Jesus follower.

Preparing a mango to serve to another may help us identify with the good Samaritan: it involves inverting the thing that holds all things together to be able to rightly taste and see what is good about the structure in the first place. Good Samaritans don't just carry a mango in their pocket; they're ready to serve it, give it away, share it for the sake of the one they find hungry, hurting, or broken.

The leathery skin of a mango is inedible. It can be used for many things, but usually it is no more than a holding chamber for the part you can eat and the part you can use to reproduce the mango: the seed. So as inedible as it is, the skin holds everything together. The skin, the structure of the fruit, becomes pliable and can even be turned inside out. Likewise, the structure of the law that we can be so rigid in keeping can do only one thing: give a framework for how the fruit inside changes it from the inside out. The outside color of a mango always tells you when it's ready. As you sit in the light of the Son, he also reveals when you are ready to follow him just like he modeled the structure of the law: they will know you by your love (John 13:35). This is the fruit, and in his upside-down kingdom, it is the law upon which all others hang.

Just as Jesus peeled the law back to two—love God and love others—so did God in the Ten Commandments. The first four are about God and how we are to love him; the last six are about us and how we are to love each other. While Jesus came not to abolish the law but rather to fulfill it, the law remained unchanged. I don't think we can even say that he simplified it, simply because there's nothing simple about loving God the way that God asks us to or about loving people the way that God commands us to.

Jesus' good Samaritan parable of a man in need focuses on one thing: love trumps law. In so doing, Jesus answers the lawyer's original question: love God and others and you will *live*. Portraying the Samaritan as the hero of the story leaves the lawyer to contend with his own evaluation of the law because good Jews should know "to act justly and to love mercy and to walk humbly with [their] God" (Micah 6:8). This story shocks the audience and defies all human boundaries of race, religion, nationality, economic class, and education. Because none of this was known. All the good Samaritan knew was that the man in the ditch needed help. And that was enough.[4] Because compassion has no boundaries, and judging people on any basis of identity may well leave us lying in a ditch.[5]

Isn't that one of the most beautiful things about Jesus? He recognizes and meets the one in front of him, in the way they're wired to learn, understand, engage. He met the lawyer with a logical argument, even though it made no sense for a Jewish man to want to be like a Samaritan.

Have you ever noticed how much we want it both ways in the church? We want to point to "the Samaritan woman" as a harlot, unfaithful, rejected, implying that somehow, being Samaritan (and all the sin that is implied) matters more than simply where Jesus found her. Yet we also want to *be* "the good Samaritan." So which is it? Is the identity of Samaritan the problem? Or was Jesus constantly overturning the prejudice of his day by showing up for real Samaritan people and also making them the hero of a story so many failed to understand?

The good Samaritan did what the religious, faithful, "clean" followers of the law refused to do. And the lawyer could not help but notice that the one who showed mercy was the one for whom *he* was least likely to have mercy. It is not lost on me that I have done nothing to deserve the mercy of Jesus. Yet here I am, covered in it, welcome to it, invited to share it radically and liberally. So who are you in the story? I've been all the characters, including the victim in the ditch. But most often, have I been the one who walked by? Have I been the one who had an excuse, a "valid" reason, a theological stake in the ground, somewhere to be, and neglected to stop to share the grace, mercy, and limitless love of Jesus? Father, forgive us. In our desire to be anything but a Samaritan, it is entirely possible that we have also been anything but good.

When we choose judgment over mercy or law over love, we make the conversation about the thing we are uncomfortable with rather than the thing that the one in front of us might need. A conversation about identity isn't the same as rescuing someone from a ditch, but a kid can certainly feel like they have been thrown in one if you lay all your "laws" on the table first. They may unchoose you as the person to have the conversation with and go looking for someone who will just help them get on their feet. Questions around identity can be disorienting for a child. Having the courage to claim one's identity can be equally dangerous for a child. You can choose, long before you are invited into the conversation, that you will show compassion first, or you can choose to step around the conversation (or the kid) because of your beliefs. Either way, your choice will be evident to the one in the parabolic ditch.

12

WHAT ARE YOU AFRAID OF? (THE BIG, HAIRY PIT)

When I first began talking about the conversation about identity in the church (yes, you read that right), I realized that I wasn't necessarily up against opposing views or rival theologies that determine one's fate to join Jesus in heaven or be convicted to a life of eternal damnation (although that was palpable in the room)—rather, I was up against fear.

About a year ago, a pastor friend bravely asked me to join him and his church for a conversation around kids, gender, sexuality, and identity. I had no connections to this congregation, and it was on the other side of the country. I think the distance and seeming anonymity made it feel safe, perhaps even for both of us. If I misspoke, I'd be headed home on Monday. If I helped, I would facilitate the beginning of something that they would be equipped to carry together.

As has always been the case in every such scenario (a workshop situation with people who read past the fact that I'm a kids' pastor and focus both my research and material around identity and emerging generations), someone wanted to talk about same-sex marriage. My usual approach is to remind the room that we are not talking about marriage, because:

a. Kids don't get married.

b. Marriage is often an idol in the church, and we do not need to position it as the ideal, let alone discuss that perspective with children. (How many of us have complicated relationships with the definition of marriage or our experience of it as a child or adult?)

c. Conversations about gender and sexuality do not need to imply marriage or define marriage (for so many reasons, not least because our social constructs of marriage have been warped and twisted by patriarchy and misogyny for centuries, so please, let's just hold our parameters loosely while those two vices loosen their grip).

d. Conversations about gender and sexuality are not the same conversation. Gender and sexuality have implications toward one another, but gender is one aspect of identity. Sexuality is another aspect of identity. (And the desire to conflate the two is usually defended by the desire to define sin. Sigh.)

My clarification that we are not talking about marriage invariably leads to a pursuit of my opinion, to which I tend to respond with some (hopefully) respectful form of "My opinion of the biblical definition of marriage is none of your business." I remind the room that I am not their pastor and am not in relationship with them, and that opinions can be damaging, unhelpful, and even toxic if voiced without the opportunity to do life together. I am usually pushed to take a stand on "the biblical definition of marriage," at which point I again refer to points a, b, c, and d. But mostly d.

If I am having a private conversation, I might be cheeky enough to ask, "Which 'biblical' definition of marriage are you referring to? Polygamy? The kind with concubines? The one where the beauty pageant winner gets to be the wife? Or maybe by biblical you mean the King James version, where the purpose of marriage for centuries, if not millennia, was the transfer of property, political and military alliances, and money or goods in exchange for a woman's (if not a girl's) hand in marriage, and love had little to do with it?"

Let's not pretend that the church has been propping up some version of Paul's poetic definition whereby a husband and wife are earthly vessels of "Christ and his bride" and the love Jesus has for his church. Church and state have done a pretty good job of defining marriage according to their own constructs and needs for thousands of years, and love was never the linchpin.

Matthew 19:4–6 does, indeed, give us Jesus' beautiful words about the ideal of marriage, and this is an important passage to consider for a conversation about marriage, if we were having that conversation. But I am asking that we do not claim this to be the standard by which marriage has historically taken place. Jesus' beautiful words imply consent, mutuality, and a loving bond. These values have been conditions of modern marriage for less than a hundred years. So we cannot point to one passage and declare, "This is the biblical definition of marriage," because it hasn't been the definition applied to marriage historically. Insisting on it today implies it has always been so. And it hasn't.

But I digress. At the gathering with my pastor friend's church, I watched a gentleman (likely in his sixties) struggle and grow increasingly emotional at my unwillingness to engage the question at hand. I listened to him speak his mind and voice his concerns, which concluded with this question: *How far are we willing to push this?* I learned so much about his perspective simply from how he worded this question and how freely he asked it (as if it was the question we were all seeking to answer). A few working assumptions were revealed, and I was able to soften my gaze, drop my shoulders, and change my pace.

1. He was acknowledging a *we*. It wasn't us versus them. It wasn't *I* or *you*. Community mattered to him, and this was his church family.

2. The use of the word *willing* implied his opinion that concessions had been made along the way, and there was a "too far" that things could be pushed. And if that happened, then what? It was the *then what* that I was curious about, and I desperately wanted to be empathetic. It also appeared that, beyond the brave face, he was afraid.

So I asked him: "What are you afraid of?"

"I'm not afraid of anything," he replied, agitated.

"Okay, so if you're not afraid, how do you define how far we've pushed this? How far is too far?"

He stumbled over his words and grew flummoxed as he waffled between "It's not fear, it's . . ." and "It's just that . . ." and "Some things are sacred." As his fists hit the table and his chin began to quiver, this lovely, God-fearing man boldly announced, "I'm afraid if we cross the line, God will remove blessing from this church." And there it was. Sitting like a giant pink elephant in the middle of the room was the truth for so many who weren't brave enough to say it out loud.

I let the elephant sit in silence for a moment or two longer than it felt comfortable to do so. I did not offer an explanation or a retort. I wouldn't assuage his fear or dismiss it, as has been my experience too many times when wrestling with big questions in faith spaces. All I could offer was truth: the words of Jesus, the wide-open arms of his love, and his invitation to just sit.

Because that is what Jesus so often did: sit. When others would walk past, jeer, pick up stones, or argue, Jesus chose to sit down, stay present, and ask questions. Let's revisit the time he sat with the woman at the well and asked her, "Will you give me a drink?"

That particular encounter often gets used to call Christians to be more like Jesus. The spin usually goes something like this:

- She was a promiscuous woman (as if the number of husbands she had was necessarily her choice). Therefore, Jesus should not have approached her. It was culturally inappropriate.
- He asked her for something (again, taboo) and started a conversation (also taboo).
- Her life was changed by this encounter with Jesus, so we shouldn't be afraid to talk to people who are rejected or displaced (more or less true, but not the point as I see it).

Here's what I think was actually going on:

- Jesus noticed a person who, likely against her will, was subjected to a life of being trafficked and traded and, as a result, had no social standing that would even allow her to change her status, let alone collect water at a more reasonable time of day.
- He asked her for the one thing—the only thing—she could offer him (and that he could not get for himself), regardless of whether it made sense. This set up an exchange that offered the woman dignity in return.

- He came to her. He didn't call her away from what she was doing or ask her to meet him at the temple sometime between nine and eleven on Saturday morning. He moved toward her and waited for an invitation to come closer and have a conversation. He gave her agency, and she consented to the exchange: water for living water.

The baseline interpretation, when we lean too heavily into the descriptors of this story, is that the woman was the lowest of the low, of ill repute, and unapproachable because of her people group (Samaritan divorcee at best), and the miracle is that Jesus would sit with "even her."

But what we actually see in this story is that those who identify differently than we do, whether by sexuality, gender, socioeconomic status, ethnicity, or otherwise, are not less than us. They may, in fact, love Jesus just as much as we do. Their relationship with Jesus is not determined by how they identify with and in the world; it is determined by how they identify in the kingdom and with the King. What we see and what they say about who they are doesn't make them a "Samaritan woman" just because we don't agree with them (and it doesn't make us Jesus in the story, either). Just like posting a sign in front of our church that says "All are welcome" doesn't mean we've done the work of walking through Samaria. But we might be operating from a bounded-set perspective if we think a person should clean themselves up (whatever that means) before they receive an invitation to walk through our doors. And if someone has to read a handbook akin to *Robert's Rules of Order* to be welcomed, accepted, and loved, we're doing it wrong.

I'm not saying that people do not sin, or that sin doesn't matter. What I am saying (again) is that discipleship happens on top of relationship, and without a relationship, our judgment of someone else's perceived sin is, quite frankly, none of their business. And if they are not in a relationship with Jesus, I would imagine they aren't particularly interested in what qualifies as sin to you or to him.

Sin has no context outside the kingdom. It's just life and choices. I am mostly afraid that we are more concerned with other peoples' sins and not concerned enough that they are not in the kingdom. Not only do we not necessarily have an invitation to speak into their life outside of kingdom context, what they do or do not do does not matter outside of relationship with Jesus. Meaning, sin is anything that separates us from God. If a person does not have a relationship with Jesus, they are already separated from God. Worry about that. Worry more about a relationship with them so that you can invite them into a relationship with Jesus and less about the things you think they need to change in order to be welcome.

In Romans 10:13–15 we read, "'Everyone who calls on the name of the Lord will be saved.' How, then, can they call on the one they have not believed in? And how can they believe in the one of whom they have not heard? And how can they hear without someone preaching to them? And how can anyone preach unless they are sent? As it is written: 'How beautiful are the feet of those who bring good news!'"

Start a conversation. Ask a question. Sit down. But if you start with a decision that the person you're looking at is anything other than beloved, back away from the well.

When we decide for others which aspects of their lives are sinful, we deny them consent, mutuality, and agency not only in our relationship with them but also in the relationship we long for them to form with Jesus. Notice that Jesus almost always begins with a question when approaching someone to whom he will offer salvation. Also notice that he often cites that it is their faith that has healed them. So even if you believe someone needs healing, they first need faith and a desire for relationship with Jesus.

So why did Jesus go through Samaria instead of around it? The truth is he went through many places and things that people had been dancing around for centuries. He came to show us and do for us what God had been inviting us into all along: loving relationship with him.

This wasn't a one-time occurrence; Jesus made a habit of going through Samaria. On one occasion, Jesus healed ten men with leprosy on his way through (Luke 17:11–19). I've heard this story told many ways, and I think we generally land on the idea that we want to be like the one who came back, "praising God in a loud voice" (v. 15), especially when teaching it to children. But as usual, there is something more worth mining for, something worth interrogating. A detail we sometimes miss in this story: the men with leprosy asked for Jesus' healing. Word had traveled, and they knew he could heal them.

Most of us want to experience healing in one form or another, or even just witness healing for someone we love. Many of us will look at someone's situation and decide what needs healing (I am not suggesting we do this; I am observing that we do, in fact, do this). When one of my kids lost her vision overnight, I prayed earnestly for her healing. Until she asked me not to. She told me that not being able to see wasn't the problem for her. The problem was my inability to accept it. "Pray for that," she said. "Ask Jesus to help you accept my blindness."

So when we look at other people's lives—including those born with ailments, who have diseases, who are neurodivergent, who identify as queer, who disagree with us or our theology—I caution us not to pray for healing over the thing we dislike, don't understand, believe needs to change, or do not have consent to bring before the Lord on behalf of another. Why? Because Jesus didn't, and we'd best follow his lead.

For example, when Jesus encountered the man on the mat by the pool in Bethesda in John 5:1–15, he asked him, "Do you want to be healed?" And with Bartimaeus, the blind man, Jesus asked, "What do you want?" (Mark 10:51). Jesus didn't declare what needed to change for either of them. Or that they should want anything to change. They declared their faith in how they answered, and they were declared healed. What if all either of them wanted was clean clothes or a hot meal? Jesus likely would have given them those things. We know he fed thousands and implored us, his followers, to take care of the poor, the hungry, and the lost. The point is, he asked.

The other thing to notice about the story of the ten men with leprosy is that the one who returned worshiped as his response. It's not simply gratitude, it's an act of worship. Few of us have the faith to understand what, or who, has truly healed us. We want the leprosy to go away, but we don't necessarily want what a life healed by faith will require of us: repentance. To turn and return. The invitation to repentance isn't just for "those" people. Just like the invitation to healing isn't only for those we think are sick. It's for you and me every day. To turn from the things of the day that distracted us from Jesus and return to him in worship. Do we want the wrong thing to be healed? Do we just want the men to stop having leprosy, or do we want their hearts, minds, and spirits healed as they step out of the world and into the kingdom of God?

Back along the border between Galilee and Samaria, we know that these ten men called Jesus "Master." They knew whom they were talking to, but they asked only for "pity," for relief from the pain and symptoms of their illness. They were sent to their priest, and somewhere along the way between here and there, they were healed. Jesus always requires faith for healing. What we don't know is whether this healing changed how they lived their lives, or whether they believed Jesus was Messiah, or whether they entered the kingdom of heaven. We just know they were healed of leprosy. That tells us who they believed Jesus to be: Healer. And it tells us they knew he could do it. It doesn't tell us about their faith beyond their desire to be healed. Let's not mistake healing for salvation.

What I do know for sure is that Jesus never asked them to change who they were or to make themselves worthy of the temple before he offered them living water, legs that work, eyes that see, or freedom from disease before he would engage with them. (Likewise, behavioral conformity, or "praying the gay away," does not a disciple make.) I also know that when they went home, they told their families and friends what Jesus had done for them, and whole communities were transformed by the good news of Jesus.

I recently heard someone talk about why the OG twelve disciples could not have been the religious cream of the crop, so to speak. For if they were, they would have been rabbis and not needed to follow one. They had jobs that tell us they were not Torah scholars. What does that tell us about whom Jesus invites close and includes in his story?

For every person that we reject because "that's pushing it too far" or "they're sinners," you know what Jesus says? He says, "Are you tired? Worn out? Burned out on religion? Come to me. Get away with me and you'll recover your life. I'll show you how to take a real rest. Walk with me and work with me—watch how I do it. Learn the unforced rhythms of grace.

I won't lay anything heavy or ill-fitting on you. Keep company with me and you'll learn to live freely and lightly" (Matthew 11:28–30 *The Message*).

Conversations about identity must be rooted in relationship. If we are going to be friends, you're probably not going to want to start with how you've amassed wealth or maybe squandered it, or not been generous, or gossiped, or hurt someone you love, or betrayed a friend, or cheated, lied, or let your anger get the best of you. I know I would prefer to not laundry-list my sins before you decide whether I'm qualified for a friendship with you. So even if you believe that same-sex marriage is a sin or think that being transgender is a choice or that some people are too far gone, I am inviting you to not sin against people by choosing to judge them before you know them. I fear that in doing so we inadvertently or intentionally disqualify them from the kingdom in the process. Our sins disqualify every single one of us. It is only the blood of Jesus and the mysterious love of a very good God that fling wide the gates of the kingdom of heaven for anyone ever. And everyone is always welcome.

So, what am I afraid of? I am afraid of a child being disqualified from the gospel, God's kingdom, and relationship with Jesus, who knows them, loves them, and receives them just as they are, because someone told them that who they say they are is wrong, willful sin, or unacceptable to God. I am afraid of children being condemned before they have been confirmed as image bearers. I am afraid that kids are walking away from Jesus because the church turned its back on them. As a disciple, my job is to make more disciples, not to decide who is a worthy disciple. None of us are worthy. All of us are invited. All of us. Even the ones with whom we disagree.

13

IS THERE ENOUGH MANGO FOR EVERYONE?

I often wonder about the stories we choose to tell children from Scripture and how we choose to tell them. Take the story of the five loaves and two fish, for example. We love to celebrate that Jesus could use "even" a boy's lunch (as in John 6:1–13) and the wild miracle of feeding five thousand men this way (not including women and children, by the way). But as I revisit these extraordinary stories of Jesus' miraculous presence, I find wonder in different parts of the story than I used to, and especially in the parts of the story we don't often talk about.

Let's consider for another moment the story of the five loaves and two fish as it appears in Mark 6:34–44:

> When Jesus landed and saw a large crowd, he had com-
> passion on them, because they were like sheep without a
> shepherd. So he began teaching them many things.
>
> By this time it was late in the day, so his disciples came
> to him. "This is a remote place," they said, "and it's already
> very late. Send the people away so that they can go to the

surrounding countryside and villages and buy themselves something to eat."

But he answered, "You give them something to eat."

They said to him, "That would take more than half a year's wages! Are we to go and spend that much on bread and give it to them to eat?"

"How many loaves do you have?" he asked. "Go and see."

When they found out, they said, "Five—and two fish."

Then Jesus directed them to have all the people sit down in groups on the green grass. So they sat down in groups of hundreds and fifties. Taking the five loaves and the two fish and looking up to heaven, he gave thanks and broke the loaves. Then he gave them to his disciples to distribute to the people. He also divided the two fish among them all. They all ate and were satisfied, and the disciples picked up twelve basketfuls of broken pieces of bread and fish. The number of the men who had eaten was five thousand.

Here are a few places in this passage where I find wonder:

1. Jesus' compassion for the people in the crowd is likened to one compelled to caring for sheep without a shepherd. If I've learned anything about shepherding from Jesus, it's that sheep are very vulnerable without a shepherd. And shepherds lead their sheep to what they need: food, water, shelter, safety, rest.

2. The disciples are not compassionate. They are overwhelmed by an irrational ask, and their response is understandable. I think we are often hard on a bunch of dudes who react in ways that are not unlike how we might react today if asked to do something that feels impossible.

3. The reactions of the disciples (and our likely reactions if we were put in the same position) seem to come from the

scarcity framework out of which we often operate: there is not enough. If I share what I have, give it away, or let you have my portion, I will lack what I need. Even though the Bible is full of promises to the contrary, even though Jesus proves the sufficiency of his grace over and over, even though God meets the needs of God's people over and over again. God's sufficiency is lavish generosity, modeled by a child.

4. There were leftovers.

This idea that the opposite of scarcity is sufficiency (rather than abundance) highlights what the disciples could have expected from Jesus at this point: enough. God promises enough. Jesus asks us to let today's worries be enough (Matthew 6:34). There is manna for today, and once a week, enough for two days so you can rest (Exodus 16). The Western understanding of scarcity and the ensuing understanding of prosperity have created a misunderstanding of the lavish nature of sufficiency. When we use the word *lavish*, we mean extravagant, excess. But isn't the very definition of extravagant generosity found in God's meeting our needs? Our culture would have us believe that gluttony is lavish, that more-than-enough is just enough, and that generosity looks like wealth. What God says is enough is more than enough, because God is the one who "is able to do immeasurably more" than we ask or imagine (Ephesians 3:20). We can't begin to grasp what extravagance looks like in the kingdom if we have not grasped the lavishness of God's *sufficient* provision.

However, I think we get close to understanding "immeasurably more" when we pay attention to how Jesus loves. He didn't decide who was hungry enough or needed an extra measure of compassion. He didn't separate people into groups and say, "Those who haven't sinned can have supper," or "Those who are the most hungry eat first." He didn't feed only men.

No one was excluded from the meal. No one was rejected from his table. No one was judged, measured, or lined up against a definition of worthiness before getting not just food but *enough* food. This is the love of Jesus.

So I wonder: If we get to feast at his table and there is enough for everyone, why do we think we get to decide who gets a basket? How does one have to behave before getting fed? From whom do we withhold an invitation to the feast out of fear of there being enough? There is enough for all people. There is plenty for each of God's created ones. There is lavish sufficiency in each helping of love poured out on each of us, so much so that we have been granted access to the source and can pour it all out in a day and be filled again by morning. You can give away God's love, the very essence of Jesus, as much and as often as you are able and know that there is enough and you will not be left empty. You do not have to decide how to group people, where they should sit, who gets to be where, or how close to Jesus one group should be over another. You simply get to invite anyone and everyone to feast on the five loaves and two fish and watch Jesus do the rest.

Bring your modest lunch and watch what God can do. I promise you, you will not go without. You will not go hungry because you shared. God will not withhold from you. And God does not withhold love from anyone. But if people don't know there's enough, they might pass the basket by. So tell your neighbor, your kids, your friends, your church, and your family that there is enough, no matter how hungry they are, no matter how hungry they say they are, and no matter how hungry you think they should be. There is enough.

"Do not withhold good from those to whom it is due, when it is in your power to act" (Proverbs 3:27). From what I can tell, good is due to all.

TODAY'S MANGOES AND TODAY'S PARENTS (REAL TALK FOR THE CHURCH)

*A **note to parents:** The research presented in this chapter is meant to help support those in your church community as they endeavor to understand how to have this conversation with you so that you feel supported in having it with your kids. I invite you to think through your own spirituality and beliefs and how they influence your parenting. The hope is that you will also better understand the reality your churches are facing as they, too, navigate the tensions and truths in this conversation.*

According to many research projects, ages zero to sixteen is the fastest declining demographic in the church. The "nones" category of adults (those with no religious affiliation) has increased, and discipleship is currently the hot topic at most churches. Whose job is it to lead kids spiritually? How can the church do so if the kids aren't there? And how can the parents be expected to lead their kids spiritually if they themselves are struggling to walk as disciples, if they even are disciples?

What we know for sure is that kids are rarely the decision-makers for how or where (or if) they end up at church on Sunday. Who is missing from the church community, and how do we create a space that welcomes and includes today's parents so that we can walk with them through the spiritually formative years of their children's lives? Do they feel safe engaging with a church after their own experience? Are they concerned about how their child or children may be received?

For those of us committed to ministry to kids, focusing on the parents' demographic helps us better understand what matters to today's parents and what we can do to invite them into the community and grow in relationship with us. So, who is today's parent, and how are they choosing church? How can we equip parents and support this generation of kids? And where are the new opportunities—and how can we, the church, create them for them?

WHO ARE TODAY'S PARENTS?

Every year, I like to take a look at the Deloitte Global Gen Z and Millennial Annual Survey[1] to get a glimpse of the decision-making drivers in the lives of today's economic engine—millennials and older members of Gen Z, or for the purposes of this chapter, today's parents.

While I'm not sure I had a handle on economics as a child (or do today), I remember hearing words like *recession*. I remember my family losing our house and cars one year. I remember the shift in my understanding between wants and needs. And I remember very unhelpful euphemisms like "Stay under the spout where the glory comes out" spoken over us in the singsong tones of the pastor's wife, serving us some twisted version of the prosperity gospel. For the record, if that's how glory works, it must be mango juice in the pipes.

As the church, we get to come alongside people no matter what they're facing, no matter how they got there, no matter where they started, no matter whether you agree with them or not. And parents are coming to us with all kinds of concerns: mental health challenges; missed developmental milestones and medical diagnoses; the cost of living, including groceries, housing, and gas; civil unrest and war on multiple continents; unemployment; school tensions; bullying. All of this is at the top of mind of parents before we even get to a conversation about identity. Parents are living in a "it's not supposed to be this way/this hard/this far from what I planned" season. And the season doesn't seem to be changing.

Here's what Deloitte's 2023 survey executive summary reveals (it's very similar to 2022, but cost of living concerns are likely only higher after 2023):

> [While] satisfaction with work/life balance and employer progress on DEI [diversity, equity, and inclusion], societal impact, and environmental sustainability have improved, . . . the majority remain unimpressed with businesses' societal impact overall. . . . The high cost of living is their top societal concern, with unemployment and climate change ranking second and third. Half of Gen Zs and millennials say they live paycheck to paycheck. . . . Gen Zs and millennials are responding to financial pressures by taking on side jobs (on the rise compared to 2022), postponing big life decisions like buying a house or starting a family, and adopting behaviors that save money (and help the environment) such as buying second-hand clothes or not driving a car.[2]

Let me interpret some of this data for you: This generation of families is struggling. Parents need support not only in the spiritual formation of their kids (and themselves), but also in getting through the week. They have less to offer financially, and they have less time to give because they are working multiple jobs, some without reliable transportation to get there. In other words, they're not necessarily truant from church; they're desperate to make ends meet. Perhaps they need us to meet them in Samaria instead of requiring them to show up at the temple in Jerusalem.

The survey summary continues:

> Gen Zs and millennials are rethinking the role of work in their lives. While 49% of Gen Zs and 62% of millennials say work is central to their identity, work/life balance is something they are striving for. Having a good work/life balance is the top trait they admire in their peers, and their top consideration when choosing a new employer. . . . However, most don't feel that reducing their hours would be a realistic option as they can't afford the pay cut it would require. Gen Zs and millennials clearly value remote and hybrid work and see its benefits. Three-quarters of respondents who are currently working in remote or hybrid roles would consider looking for a new job if their employer asked them to go on-site full-time.[3]

It's possible that they feel the same way about church. Online community *is* community for this generation of families, and while many would prefer to ditch the online service we rushed to manifest during the pandemic, what if it is the well, the place where Jesus meets with some, simply because it's the place they can show up to at a time when they can give their full attention?

Taking this further, today's kids learn on screens (according to a 2020 report by Common Sense Media, nearly half of

kids ages two to four and more than two-thirds of kids ages
five to eight have their own mobile device[4]). Kids need better
on-screen options. Parents are looking for quality program-
ming for their kids that helps them raise up this generation to
be confident in who they are so that they can change the world
for the better. That sounds a lot like a gospel mandate, even
if they don't know it yet. And if a mobile device can deliver
a case of mangoes to my house with a few clicks, why are
we finding it so challenging to deliver sweet, rich, beautiful
Jesus-centered content the same way?

The Deloitte survey continues:

> Stress and anxiety levels remain high, and burnout is on the
> rise: Nearly half of Gen Zs (46%) and four in 10 millenni-
> als (39%) say they feel stressed or anxious at work all or
> most of the time. Their longer-term financial futures, day-
> to-day finances, and the health/welfare of their families are
> top stress drivers, while concerns about mental health and
> workplace factors such as heavy workloads, poor work/life
> balance, and unhealthy team cultures are also at play. Gen
> Zs and millennials are reporting increasingly high levels of
> burnout due to work-related pressures.[5]

In other words, work is central to the identity of Gen Zs
and millennials, but they are burning out. So how can we
help? The gospel offers us a way to come alongside those
who are weary, burdened, and burned out on religion, and it
may be that a better conversation about identity could serve
families holistically. Equipping families to gather around the
kitchen table with different parameters to measure who we
are and how we show up in the world offers us the opportunity to regroup, reframe, and rethink what we will center
on, together. And if who we are is found in who Jesus is first,

helping parents reorient their identity better equips them for a conversation with their kids.

"Harassment in the workplace is a significant concern, particularly for Gen Zs," the Deloitte report notes.

> More than six in 10 Gen Zs (61%) and around half of millennials (49%) have experienced harassment or microaggressions at work in the past 12 months. Inappropriate emails, physical advances, and physical contact are the most common types of harassment, while exclusion, gender-based undermining and unwanted jokes are the most common types of microaggressions. Of those who experienced harassment, around eight in 10 reported it to their employer, however, a third of Gen Zs and a quarter of millennials don't think the issues were handled effectively. Women, non-binary, and LGBT+ respondents are less likely to report harassment to their employer and less likely to feel their organization responded well.[6]

Let me cut to the chase on this one: if you think that the same is not true in church contexts, you are part of the privileged majority and you would be wrong. The word *sanctuary* is supposed to mean something. Your church was built with the intention of safety to worship, to gather, to celebrate, to study. If it is not safe for all people to enter and find Jesus, it is not safe.

Finally, the survey notes that climate change

> is a major concern for Gen Zs and millennials, but finances are making it harder for them to prioritize sustainability. Concerns about climate change have a major impact on their decision-making, from family planning and home improvements, to what they eat and wear, to career and

workplace choices. Gen Zs and millennials are taking action on climate change, with seven in 10 respondents saying they actively try to minimize their impact on the environment. Financial concerns may put a damper on these efforts; more than half of respondents think it will become harder or impossible to pay more for sustainable products and services if the economic situation stays the same or worsens.[7]

If I rephrase "climate change" as "creation care," does that help give a pathway to partnership with this generation of movers and shakers? Consider your church's carbon footprint: What is your community doing to prioritize creation care? How might that impact engagement with today's families? What the survey respondents are saying is this: When we buy cheap (because that's what we can afford, or because that's good "stewardship"), it often comes at a cost that cannot be measured in dollars. Millennials and members of Gen Z would rather see churches use less stuff, which includes acknowledging climate change, minimizing waste, and eliminating single-use plastic. This tells them not only who you are as a community, but also that what matters to them matters to you, too. And the planet needs to matter. It's God's most phenomenal gift to us, and God asked us to take care of it. Today's parents know we've made a mess of it, and they'd like to be part of the solution for their kids' futures.

How can our knowledge and understanding of these trying realities inform how we engage with and equip today's parents? How can we pay attention to these concerns and walk with parents in and through them in such a way that we build discipleship pathways through relationship, empathy, and compassion? What can we learn from their voiced and *global* concerns? How can we meet them where they are and move toward the well (instead of asking them to move toward us)? And parents, we want to hear from you. We need to know what you need. We may not have all the answers, but we certainly want to support you as you navigate the realities that you and your kids are facing.

WHAT DOES THIS TELL US THAT PARENTS CARE ABOUT? (WHAT ARE THEIR MANGOES?)

Equipping people spiritually begins with building a community that cares about what matters to them. Earlier, I wrote that God's kingdom is all about God meeting our needs. When was the last time you asked a parent, "What do you need, and how can I help?"

Here are some things to consider:

- Where can parents in your context easily find community?
- Are there any barriers?
- How can you leverage what matters to parents?
  - o How can you support the financial concerns that parents are facing?
  - o Are there programs you can offer, like a parent's night out or a Bible study with free childcare that meets in the neighborhood instead of at the church?
  - o Does the church reflect creation care in a way that mirrors millennial and Gen Z concern for sustainability and climate change?
  - o Are there classes or experts you can bring in to discuss mental health, common challenges, coping strategies, identity, or topics that parents and kids are navigating? Have you asked parents what sort of classes they would benefit from? And can you

offer them at times that work for families even if it's inconvenient for church staff?

How we choose to acknowledge, learn from, and engage with the knowledge that such research surveys can provide will be an indicator of whether we have access to today's kids and families. We have not earned the right to speak into their values, their priorities, let alone their definitions of identity, if we have not created a safe space to have real talk about the things that matter to them. And if we read between the lines of the Deloitte study, the things that matter to these most highly educated generations also matter to God: the planet, our mental health, poverty, work-life balance (aka Sabbath).

In order to properly introduce someone to mango, that person needs to be in the same room as the mango. The senses matter to the experience. How can you respond to what Gen Z and millennials are telling us the world over, with mango in hand, even if it means going through Samaria?

15

HOW DO YOU GET INTO THIS THING?

When it comes to how best to reach and engage kids in these important conversations, most of us would agree that growing in understanding and compassion for what kids, youth, parents, and those who love them and lead them are facing, and meeting them where they are, needs to be a top priority.

But then we arrive at a sticking point: According to a 2022 Barna Group study, when asked "Where should the primary source of children's discipleship take place?," 95 percent of children's ministry leaders said it should be at home—and 51 percent of parents of kids ages five to fourteen said it should be at church.[1] We are looking at each other and assuming the other party either has it figured out or is at least responsible. I think this gap is telling us that we need to journey alongside each other as disciples for the sake of the spiritual formation of this generation of kids.

WHAT WE NEED TO KNOW, IN ORDER TO BEGIN

By the age of five, children have formed an idea of who or what they think God is. This is a time of discovery. Throughout childhood (roughly between ages five and twelve), kids will decide whether what they believe about God is true. During this time, many decisions are made about faith, belief, and choosing to be a Jesus follower. The Barna study notes that a person's worldview is primarily shaped and firmly in place by the time a person is thirteen. And throughout adolescence until the age of seventeen, youth will defend their decisions and make other decisions accordingly. We've all witnessed this: the defensive posture of a teenager firmly committed to, and advocating for, their beliefs, values, and understanding of the world around them, notwithstanding how faith intersects with these.

So what does this tell us? If Scripture is one big story about who God says God is *and* about who God says we are, kids of all ages need to know the truth about both from a young age in order for their spiritual identity to firmly root the fullness of their identity.

WHAT EQUIPPING NEEDS DO WE NEED TO CONSIDER?

First, the gospel was meant to be accessible and unhindered. The language we use can be the very hindrance we are trying to avoid (see Acts 28:30–31). Yet the language of the church (words that are scriptural and not daily or social vernacular) can create a sense of exclusion for families who do not yet know the language of Scripture. This is not to say that words like *gospel*, *sin*, *salvation*, *baptism*, and *discipleship* don't matter; rather, they need context and deserve careful exegesis so that those who already understand are invitational rather than exclusionary in how they talk about Jesus, God's love for us, and the invitation to be part of the body. (That last sentence is exactly what I'm talking about. We talk about the body of Christ, and kids may think we mean his actual body. We want them to know he had a real body. We also want them to understand Paul's metaphor of being part of one body of Jesus followers as in 1 Corinthians 12.)

Further, we cannot assume that all grownups understand this language. Not all parents are disciples yet. Not all parents are Christians, even if they show up on a Sunday. Not everyone inside the church was raised in the church as a child. Their values, character, and morals may have developed in a different context. When we make assumptions about how we should talk about any topic (including faith), we discount individual, unique contributions and experiences. If we admit that some parents are just as new to Jesus as their kids, we may need to equip family members to walk beside each other (instead of parents out in front). In the same way that a conversation is an exchange, family discipleship today may require an unprecedented mutuality as families learn, together, how to follow Jesus. As we equip for a conversation that makes space for a child to not only listen and learn but also lead at times, we model what Jesus may have been teaching when he said, "Let the little children come to me, and do not hinder them, for the kingdom of heaven belongs to such as these" (Matthew 19:14).

Also important: Building a more hopeful imagination for the nontraditional (nuclear) family. There are all kinds of definitions of family for today's kids, and I wonder if we can be creative about how we use the word *family* and, by so doing, get closer to a definition of God's radically diverse and inclusive family. Do you have an imagination for the family that arrives and is made up of two married dads and two adopted children? Have you thought through what it looks like to love them like Jesus does? Have you made space for the possibility of God's immense love for this family that welcomes them before judging them? To be clear: This is not an uncommon definition of "family." Kids have friends in families just like this one. Are families of diverse definition (whether blended, single-parent, adoptive, or foster families or families with same-sex parents or divorced parents or trans individuals, to name a few) welcome in your community? What does your conversation with Jesus sound like when you pray for your kids' friends and families?

I ask because most church-goers who were raised in the church presume that all people had access to the gospel as a child, somehow made a choice to defy it, and have found themselves back in the church as parents. So the real question is: Can you imagine a family entering your doors that has never met Jesus, and do you know how to welcome them when they're not like you?

Kids need the gospel because Jesus is the only way for them to know who they were always made to be. There is no higher value for today's parents, who value authenticity, truth, inclusion, and equity. They also value the diversity that true self-expression involves. Helping kids find their place of belonging in the body of Christ matters to Jesus, but finding belonging at all, just as they are, matters to their grownups, too. As we have explored, *identity* is a big word that means many things to each of us. As the church, helping families find their identity in Jesus and in the family of God needs to be a priority (for any generation). Equipping the adults with the language and knowledge to help today's kids find their identity as image bearers in the kingdom is careful and necessary work, but it cannot be at the cost of denying who they say they are. You may place greater value on who God says they are, but listening—*really listening*—to who they say they are is a privilege. How you define identity for today's families needs to leave space for them to share how they define it, too. Allowing for some breathing room has the potential to move us from a black-and-white conversation that polarizes people to a grey space with room for unknowns and uncertainty, and even for disagreement while still choosing unity.

Finally, we cannot preach a need for Jesus that resolves earthly tensions. Many kids (most of the world's kids, in fact) have deep, real, felt needs. Others may not understand need at all, because they have more than enough, and even their wants are attended to. Our need for Jesus is to truly know who we were made to be, as image bearers, as authentic selves, as children of God. Start here with the gospel, and watch parents and children grow equally curious about their need for Jesus, their need to know one another better, and their need for God's love.

THEOLOGICAL GUIDEPOSTS (A RECIPE FOR A BETTER CONVERSATION)

My curiosity around the conversation of identity in the church has continued to be fueled by that question I often ask in the middle of the conversation itself: What are we afraid of? What's behind what I am seeing, hearing, sensing when rooms grow quiet or agitated or confused? So I wonder if we can simply have a better conversation, with the freedom to ask such questions on purpose, facilitating a posture of listening and learning without the need to land on a side or even know in advance where it will go. Because I've been asked that question, too: Which side am I on?

We live in a polarizing culture, pitting one idea against another, assuming that any disagreement is binary. But let me gently remind you that binary thinking is simply bounded-set theology: right or wrong, in or out, black or white. Polarity denies grey. Polarity insists on one answer being correct. Polarity does not allow for diversity, equity, or inclusion of human expression or creativity or even a spectrum of possibility in between. Polarizing ideologies do not just separate ideas; they divide communities.

The hope in offering these theological guideposts is simply that we might be aware of our default postures and adjust accordingly so that we might choose to see the kids in front of us as God's own beloveds first. Even if you feel like you're sitting directly opposite the one in front of you, you get to decide how much distance you're willing to travel for the sake of this conversation. As the adult, you get to decide whether you walk toward the well and sit down, or not.

The guideposts can help us see what needs to shift in us to better steward the hearts, stories, even identities of those we get invited to sit with. These guideposts can help us discern what distance is up to us to travel *for the privilege* of sitting with someone and having this conversation, and how we can honor their courage to invite us close. They can prepare us to model the heart of God, the ways of Jesus, and the embodiment of the Holy Spirit by choosing to have eyes to see, ears to hear, hearts moved to beat in rhythm with God's, and feet fit with the peace of a very good gospel to move toward them.

The gospel is all about relationship. It always has been. It's not about a transaction or a moment. Inviting people into a relationship with Jesus has to start with their inviting us into a relationship with them first. And the foundation of any relationship is poured by trusting Jesus to handle his beloveds according to his will and God's plan for them as imagers[1] and imaginers. Do we trust the Holy Spirit enough to do what only the Spirit can do? Do we trust the Holy Spirit to use us according to her will rather than our own to fix, convince, or steer a conversation? Do we trust the Spirit enough to focus on what she equips us for and nothing more, but certainly nothing less? Our call is to invite, include, and intercede.

To be honest, it's hard to be the inviter, the sitter, or the one whom kids choose to ask the hard questions if we are afraid of the conversation we might be required to have. The grownups I encounter share common fears around the identity conversation: the fear of getting it wrong, the fear of not knowing the answers, and the fear that God will remove God's blessing from *us* if we get it wrong. I know in this moment it may seem trite to share this truth, but it might do us well to remember that perfect love does cast out fear (1 John 4:18). That there really is no condemnation for those who are in Christ Jesus (Romans 8:1). That God truly is love (1 John 4:16). By tucking away truths of Scripture to help assuage your own fears, you prevent fear itself from having a voice in your conversation.

This is where the invitation is no longer yours to give, but rather yours to receive. Perhaps you have been the inviter of kids for years. You have hosted them, celebrated them, shared with them. Yours is the house where they show up and hang out. Maybe you have been inviting the kids you love to know and love Jesus for as long as you can remember. You are now invited to trust that God knows this and honors those relationships and trusts you to have tough conversations because of the groundwork already done. You are invited to know and believe that God has gone ahead of you in every conversation *and* is simply inviting you to join in on what the Spirit has already started. What an invitation!

There comes a time when we get to release a child to invite us in. They get to choose with whom they will walk the next leg of the pilgrimage. They will do the inviting. Because this leg of the journey is about discovery and self-actualization, and the decision is not only up to them to begin, but also requires their agency, consent, a long-suffering patience, and gentleness for themselves and from those they invite.

As you watch the kids you love walk this out, I invite you to position yourself in their world to receive an invitation. Make space for them to be brave and invite you, and be willing to go at their pace. Be available so that they might be assured in advance of the offer that your RSVP will be an exuberant yes. This conversation is a long walk, not a sprint, so allow the pace to reflect that. And may your response to the invitation be as unconditional as the one you received from Jesus once upon a time.

A LONG WALK IN THE SAME DIRECTION

It was October, and I was on a pilgrimage along St. Cuthbert's Way toward Holy Island (also called Lindisfarne) in the United Kingdom. A few of us were traveling together in the group, and two of us had brought our twelve-year-olds. I had decided this was an incredible opportunity to get to know mine, to spend time and explore the world with her. And the only problem with this idea was that *I decided*. In other words, I invited her, and I also decided she was coming with me (some invitation). She was not thrilled about going, so *I* decided that *we* were going anyway. I told myself she would change her mind. She would love it and have memories that she would cherish one day. Does anyone else make decisions this way? Just me? ("She doesn't know what she's saying no to! She'll thank me later!")

Truthfully, *I* wanted time with *her*. As a twelve-year-old, my daughter was quiet but had big ideas and strong opinions, and I thought it would just be amazing to have a hundred kilometers and a whole week to just talk and ask questions and hang out. And that plan of mine *would* be amazing—if my child was extroverted, liked to chat, and wanted to hang out. But having already decided (and without her consent), we went anyway.

As we set out on our first day of walking, my daughter was immediately well ahead of me. She is taller than me and has legs that start at her armpits, so either one of us was going to have to change our pace or I was going to have to let her go on ahead.

It turns out that no matter which direction you're traveling, Scotland is always uphill. It was along one of the first gentle slopes that I looked up and realized that it didn't bother my daughter that I wasn't near. It didn't cause her any fear or concern. It didn't make her stop and wait. I was praying and had worship tunes blasting into my earbuds (I believe the song playing was Taya's "Mercy"—a fitting soundtrack to the moment), and I fell. I didn't trip, it wasn't dramatic or photo-worthy, I just fell to my knees. I was so overwhelmed by both sadness that this journey was not going to go the way I wanted and anxiety about what to do about that. I ugly cried right there on the side of the hill and just waited for the Holy Spirit to speak. I had no reason to move. I wasn't going to catch up with my kid, so I just waited.

Feeling quite sorry for myself, I mustered up the courage to ask, "What is it, Lord? What am I missing?" And as gentle and kind as the Holy Spirit has always been to me, she replied, "Let her go." The Spirit repeated the words in a whisper as I cried, and after enough repetition, my perception of the moment began to shift. There are a few ways to hear those words, "Let her go," and I absolutely heard them in the most egregious way first: "Let her go, let it go, drop the rope," where the active verb is *go* and it's hers to do.

The second and sweet way that began to cut through the noise of the enemy's taunts was allow, enable, empower her to go, and the active verb was *let*. It was mine to own, to hold, to imagine, and a gift I could give her—the thing I could do for her rather than the thing it felt like she was taking from me. The invitation in the shift was to champion what I was seeing: a strong kid with a will and a capacity for adventure who did not require me to lead. I was seeing that she didn't need me like I thought she did (or wanted her to) and that if I didn't pay attention, I would never know what she needed, because I would be too busy missing what had already passed.

I got to my feet and hit replay on "Mercy" by Taya (because I needed more) and allowed the words to wash over me before anything else. As I began to pick up the anthem and sing along (I'm sure it sounded as good as anyone singing along to earbuds, but it sounds like heaven in my memory), what I saw as I looked at the back of my daughter moving away from me had been transformed. This wasn't a grief-stricken moment; this was a miracle moment. I was staring at the back of a child with the confidence and courage to trek on, to not turn back, to explore, to lead. Where she lined up in our pack had nothing to do with me and everything to do with how God had wired her for adventure. And if I'm honest, I should have recognized it a lot sooner. I wonder how many people have only ever seen my back on a journey.

The Holy Spirit didn't let me off the hook for the rest of the week—she whispered where I would have chosen to shout, set my pace and slowed my chase, and reintroduced me to the possibility of a long walk in the same direction rather than ragged connect-the-dots pieced together by jagged fits and turns. And on our way to Holy Island, the map was laid out before me.

An average day at Lindisfarne generally does not include full sun. (Few days anywhere in the United Kingdom include full sun, to be fair.) The day we were expected to cross the channel, the forecast included fog, rain, and poor visibility. Yet as we stood on the eastern shore of the mainland and looked across to Holy Island, we could see every guidepost between here and there, glistening as bright sunshine bounced off the wet wood, with a rainbow off to one side. This made the barefoot trek ahead, across the bed of the North Sea, so clear and direct. Normally, you would see as far as the nearest guidepost and move in that direction until the next one came into view. But on this day, they could all be seen like sentinels lined up, holding post, leading the way.

There is a big difference between guideposts and guardrails. Guardrails imply speed, risk, danger, a need for narrow protection, and warning. Guardrails are preventive. Guardrails keep you within the boundaries, able to travel only within the lanes provided. Guideposts show the way, leaving the space on either side wide open. It's not that they're mere suggestions by contrast; it's just that guideposts protect by pointing the way rather than not keeping you from what isn't the way. Guideposts lead you to where you are going; guardrails keep you from going where you're not supposed to be.

We need to decide: Are we trying to prevent something, or are we trying to guide kids toward something else?

You are meant to fix your eyes in the direction of a guidepost; if you watch the guardrails, you are sure to be distracted and head the wrong direction (and for certain trouble!). So many conversations with kids sound like "Don't look at the guardrails. Don't head toward them. Don't climb over them. Stay focused on this single lane, and don't get distracted by what's on the other side. Never mind that, it isn't for you."

And while this is sound advice for a fast-moving car traveling in the same direction as other fast-moving vehicles on a highway, it doesn't work as well for the rest of life. It does not allow for the pace of a long walk, or a conversation. There's nowhere to pull over, take in the view, or wonder. It would not make sense if you walked along the shoulder of a road and paused to look over the guardrail and ask, "Why do you think this guardrail is here?" We know why it's there. But guardrails aren't for pilgrims. They're for drivers. And this life of discipleship is a pilgrimage, not the Indy 500.

We seem to be having two types of conversations with kids: ones with guardrails and others with guideposts.

Let's slow down for a moment. I want you to know that I understand why it feels right and important to throw up guardrails on either side of our kids. I get it. Life feels like it's moving too fast, things are changing at an untenable rate, and if we can protect them from what may harm them, they will stay the course. You and I both know how many accidents happen because there's something beautiful just beyond the guardrails on a bridge and our gaze wanders, or because we take a corner too fast.

So let's set a different pace for our kids. Let's not rush. Let's not worry so much about what's on the right or left. Let us fix our eyes on Jesus and keep moving in his direction. Let's choose the footpath over the highway every chance we get because the problem is often not what's beyond the guardrail; it's the pace with which we approach it.

Being a grownup for a kid includes seeing what they can't yet see. We also understand that what we are looking at may appear differently to us. And different does not necessarily mean better or clearer. Sometimes it's just different. When we remember the ways of Jesus, we realize that they always include going together.

Jesus had three common ways to engage those around him: he asked questions, he told stories, and he quoted Scripture. His questions were curious; his stories were layered with

meaning yet easily imagined; he used Scripture to remind others who they were and who God is. So when we see risk ahead,
I wonder what our kids see. Are we asking?

In all that we do, we can choose to walk in the ways of Jesus
and not simply talk about Jesus. Out on St. Cuthbert's Way,
four consistent features captured my attention: waymarkers,
fences, signs, and wide-open spaces. These features created a
sense of safety, but also a sense of security, helping us know
we were headed in the right direction or where we were meant
to be on the map.

Waymarkers, fences, signs, and wide-open spaces are helpful in navigating our conversations around identity as well.
Let's take a look at what they are and how they can help us set
out in the right direction.

WAYMARKERS
- Mark the *path*.
- *Point* to Jesus.

Mark the path

If you are wandering through the fields and hills of Scotland, I
can tell you that you'd prefer big signs to waymarkers, which
are typically a small, subtle symbol or marker indicating that
you're on the right path. There were times in the dense fog
that I would have absolutely preferred air traffic wands! As
caregivers, parents, teachers, or leaders of kids and teens, we
know that signs are easier to see and harder to ignore. But
imagine how the lush landscape would be transformed with
the intrusion of giant billboards reading "THIS WAY!"

The fear of losing one's way can cause self-doubt. We can
forget that not only do we have a map, but the path has been
walked for thousands of years, and we need not be afraid. But

also: waymarkers are small, they're the same color as weathered wood, and they are terribly infrequent. It's easy to wonder whether you're still on the right track. At some point on the Holy Island journey, we realized we were following each other and trusting that "someone" was looking for the waymarkers.

Too often, we mistake the goal as "getting it right" instead of "getting there," and as a result, we monitor every footstep instead of the direction. We arrive at the worst-case scenario too quickly and then spend our energy warning about this possible (if even unlikely) scenario. But from what I could tell on our long walk, the kids weren't looking for danger; they weren't bear hunting or looking for cliffs to fall off of. They were walking along the path, which would lead to the next waymarker. Kids generally aren't looking for ways to get into trouble. They're looking for permission to try, to have ideas, to explore, and to ask questions.

Like guideposts, waymarkers gently remind us what we're looking for and also confirm that we are headed in the right direction. More than anything, even when our kids take in the view in multiple directions, we want them to turn and return to God's plan for their lives. Looking around and knowing that there are other ways isn't the problem. The problem is not making Holy Island (so to speak) compelling enough to stay the course. And this is not achieved by making them afraid of everywhere else or denying that there is anything else out there.

We can set out waymarkers for kids and celebrate when they're on the right track. This looks like giving them enough direction, enough support, so that they don't feel alone even if they wander and explore. It looks like creating a safe space for them to come back to you when they make a mistake, when they're scared or hurting, and reminding them who they are and whose they are. What if we trusted that they want to arrive, to get it right, and to feel affirmed just as much (if not more) than we want that for them? What if *we are the way-markers*? When we create safety in the space we offer or they need, they know they can find us when they need us.

An important part of this is how we handle Scripture with kids. When we tell the tales of God's family like superhero stories and fairy tales, we run the risk of communicating two fallacies about God's Word: that it's a collection of independent stories, and that we are not among the characters in it. Teaching kids the Bible well is showing them how every piece of Scripture is tied to the whole; how nothing stands alone. The Bible is one story. We can tell stories one at a time, but not one story is isolated from a greater vision for us all.

Why does this matter? Because if we continue to isolate the Old Testament from the New, we miss out on the miraculous fulfillment of prophecy that is the life of Jesus. We miss out on how God has always led and always made a way for us to be in relationship with him. And we miss out on the fact that the Bible ends, but the story isn't over. It is in this truth that we find ourselves living out the unwritten books of Scripture. And it's only in these pages that today's kids can find themselves. They get to be part of God's story. We are in the middle of God's story, and because of Jesus, *all* are welcome to play a part in the next chapter.

Point to Jesus

Our job is not to make sure kids can retell the stories of Scripture but to know who authored them. Rather than pointing to the details of a story, highlighting its zany features or the choices of the people, using Scripture to point to Jesus looks like showing children how every moment of Scripture points to a God whose love knows no limits. Consider, for example, the story of Noah: rather than emphasize details like the type of wood Noah used to build the ark, we can help kids see that Noah, despite bullying, mockery, and any seeming earthly sense, would listen to and follow the God he loved with his whole life.

What waymarkers do you want kids to recognize when navigating tough questions and conversations with peers or differences in views, opinions, or values? Try 2 Corinthians 5:14–21 as a starting point ("For Christ's love compels us . . .") and see what bubbles out of the passage for you. Ask your kids to do the same, and stay curious.

FENCES
- *Peace* is presence.
- Fences serve a *purpose*.

Peace is presence

What does peace have to do with fences? When my kids were little, having a fenced backyard was a great source of peace for me. I could let them outside to play, to dig in the garden, to run around and know that they would still be there when it was time to come in. A fence set a boundary for how far my kids could roam without getting lost or stuck, and it gave me the freedom to not need to watch their every move. Fences also keep out unwanted animals, people, or activity from our yards or from our sight. Fences often give us peace of mind as parents or guardians of children.

But what do we tell kids about peace? What do we say to each other, let alone to kids, in a world that is riddled with injustice, oppression, inequity, war, hatred, division, about *peace*? I recently heard a local minister preach on the topic, and what he said has echoed in my thoughts ever since: "Peace is not so much about the absence of something as it is about a presence."

He's right: we often describe peace as a feeling or a sense when something difficult ends, or when we experience freedom from something that weighed us down. It is the antidote to the thing that causes us restlessness, stress, or conflict. Peace is often described as an absence of the thing that robs us of peace. Moreover, peace is the presence of Eden. Things are not as God intended them to be from the very beginning: walking around sharing presence with God.

But the minister pressed into the idea that peace is a presence. When peace shows up, he suggested, it takes over as it enters. It takes up all the extra space in a room and exhales on all in its presence. Sometimes we can be not fighting and still not be peaceful. An absence of war does not predicate the presence of peace.

The minister then asked us if we knew someone who just makes us feel better by showing up. I wonder if such a person comes to mind for you. You're at a social gathering, you've agreed to go, but only because you're expecting a specific someone else to be there. What is that sense that comes over you when they arrive? What is it that allows your shoulders to drop and your eyes to light up at the sight of them? Why does it matter that they are in the room?

Our peace is a person, too. Jesus, Prince of Peace, is the very person, the very essence of shalom. *Shalom* often gets translated as *peace* in English, but the Hebrew term is multifaceted and not quite so simply "peace." Beyond "absence of conflict," shalom also means completeness, soundness, and well-being. To experience shalom is to experience a sense of well-rounded well-being, to offer a presence of sound mind, and to be wholly present.

As Jesus said, "I have spoken all these things while I am still with you. But the Father will send the Friend in my name to help you. The Friend is the Holy Spirit. He will teach you all things. He will remind you of everything I have said to you. I leave my peace with you. I give my peace to you. I do not give it to you as the world does. Do not let your hearts be troubled. And do not be afraid" (John 14:25–27 NIrV).

Jesus left us with his Spirit—the very presence of the Prince of Peace himself. And he qualifies it: not as the world gives peace, for if that were so, there would be reason to be troubled and afraid. Because the world gives peace by creating a void of something else. Jesus gives peace by taking up all the space around it and leaving no room for that which peace consumes.

Shalom, or completeness, is who Jesus is. When he said, "It is finished," there was shalom even in his last breath. He completed what he was sent to accomplish and, in so doing, made the presence of his perfect peace available to all when he returned and left us a friend. That friend goes before us, takes up the space in the room, and allows us to enter in peace, knowing that Christ leaves his peace wherever he is.

For Jesus' friends, I wonder if walking around with Jesus was a little like a walk in the garden—a glimpse of what could be, or an understanding of the way it was supposed to be. I wonder if, with every step, the hem of his robe pulled back the curtain of Eden for even just a moment: God's love, God's presence, God with us, on earth as it is in heaven.

You get to be that presence for those who invite you close. For the child who scans the room, anxiously looking for their person as they arrive; for that friend you held while she told her story; for the one who came to Jesus because you sat with them and now invites others to do the same. You are the embodiment of the presence of peace by the Holy Spirit. Your presence brings Jesus' presence, and his presence is peace.

Conversations about identity are sacred. It is holy ground, agreeing with God about who is I Am and who I am because of God. Don't miss the opportunity to prioritize peace and presence over position or opinion. If you don't feel like you are or know how to be this kind of peace, take time to consider what might need to move out of the way in your life for peace to enter. God hears you. Jesus knows your pain, your wrestling, your desire to have this conversation well. Talk to God. Pray that the Prince of Peace, Jesus, the very presence of peace itself, would fill you with the peace you long to experience, not just the presence you wish to be for the kids you are journeying with.

Fences serve a purpose

What we say about the space inside the fence tells a child not just where we want them to be but why we want them to be there. The side of the fence we choose to be on tells them whether or not to believe us.

Someone recently said to me, "I will surely fail! There are so many things to get right and so much to do and not do." I asked, "What if following Jesus is more about starting to look like him and not about ceasing to be yourself? The more you look like Jesus, the more you grow to be who you were made to be." Drawing people to Jesus, centering on him, is more about becoming like him—and experiencing his presence, his peace, his protection—than it is about not doing other things. Fences are like guardrails in this way: if we focus on them, we will head toward them. Likewise, if we focus on guideposts, meant to draw our eye, our attention, and our focus, we will move in their direction. When we focus on who Jesus is, we cannot help but grow in his likeness.

Not all fences are experienced the same way. Some fences along St. Cuthbert's Way simply marked the division of land. Others were built to keep a certain flock or herd on one side or the other. None of them were meant for people, however, as there was always a way through, around, or over, marked with an arrow to keep us on our way.

On the third day of our long walk, from the other side of a bridge I was approaching and just out of sight, I heard what I will always remember as the most glorious sound of the week. It was the sound of my daughter's laughter. It had been too long since I had heard her laugh from her toes all the way to tears streaming down her face. It was like the rarely heard sound of an endangered songbird: I had almost forgotten her tune.

Of course I ran to catch up and spot the species singing her song in the wild (nature has forever been her home), and there she was flat on her back, bowled over by two gorgeous coonhounds licking her face like they'd been awaiting her arrival. To know this kid is to know her affection for animals of (almost) any description, and this moment felt like a divine appointment.

"I wish there was a way that God would show her his love on this trip," the other mom remarked, tongue firmly in cheek. The whole scene made me cry joyfully—there's really nothing like a child's uncontained laughter. My daughter petted the dogs and rolled around with them, played and wrestled with them. We all watched with such delight until she was ready to carry on. All at once, our walk had come to a grinding halt, and we were happy to wait on the moment before moving forward.

How often had I pushed past moments in the past? How often had I missed that rare birdsong because we had somewhere to be, miles to make, and things to do? But on this day, all we had to do was keep following the fence line until we arrived. What we would have missed if we hadn't stopped would have cost me the journey as a mom, and cost her a memory. (To this day, her favorites are the dogs and the sunsets.)

To her surprise, as we all began to walk, the dogs followed her. This made my daughter quite anxious, though she certainly didn't mind their company. It was the chattiest she had been all week, having full conversations with these hounds. What did she know that I didn't? What was her experience in these moments? Dare I ask?

As happened multiple times each day along the way, we came to a kissing gate. These gates aren't securely latched; the gate merely "kisses," or touches, the enclosure. We knew that these gates signaled passage for us as people, but a boundary for livestock. For my kid, it felt really important to keep the dogs on the same side of the fence as she found them. What she didn't realize was that those fences weren't for the dogs, just like they weren't for us. They were for the sheep.

All fences serve a purpose, but they aren't all to keep everything out or everything in. Knowing the purpose of a fence matters just as much as putting it up in the first place. Many fences we saw were centuries old and made of stone. The ones that had a bit of lean to them had been reinforced by wooden stakes. And the ones that weren't quite tall enough to keep the sheep from jumping over had barbed wire strung across the top, dotted with bits of fleece along the length where some had attempted to cross.

As we passed through the gate, the dogs went under the wooden slats of fence at this pass. As hard as she tried, that kid could not encourage those hounds back under the fence and home again. I watched her try, and I watched her stress mount as she wondered if she, somehow, would end up responsible for the dogs getting lost.

"It's okay," I told her. "Let them decide. They know the way home." She had a thousand what-ifs and worries until I said, "That fence isn't for them. It's okay. They know the way better than we do. And they know when it's time to turn around."

Yes, I can hear what I said. Yes, there was something for me in saying those words out loud to my own child. Yes, I heard the Holy Spirit remind me to "let her go."

At one point as we walked with our two new companions, my daughter came up to me and said, "You know, they could just be dogs. They don't have to mean God's love for me." If I was going to give permission for her to wonder and wander, I was going to have to let her have doubts. Our fences and religious absolutes do not make faith real. Imagination leads to faith. Faith leads to belief. And in this moment, she just needed to imagine that there may or may not be a spiritual element to this experience.

Allowing her to be unsure or to question what seemed so certain to the rest of us permits her to feel safe asking questions, climbing fences, and pushing back against what she's been taught is black-and-white. Making space for grey leaves room for the Holy Spirit. Did I trust the Spirit with my daughter? Did I trust the Holy Spirit to love her well even when they were "just dogs," after all?

Character develops through becoming, not simply by knowing the rules of good behavior. There was more to this walk than simply following the path; there was a trust and a deep understanding that others had gone before us. They'd learned along the way. And we learn along the way because of the trail they blazed for us to follow. Kids may follow or lead, blazing their own trail. They will also learn by climbing, crossing, and pushing past fences, borders, or boundaries. And we can watch them. Or we can go with them. Sometimes the way through is over or under, and sometimes the fence isn't for them. Have you made the way compelling enough to allow them the space to choose, to doubt, to wander without your fear building a new fence?

SIGNS
- *Protection* requires participation.
- Take time to *pause*.

Protection requires participation

As you would expect, there were dozens of signs along our weeklong walk; some were meant to protect, some were meant to warn, and others simply shared useful or historical information.

You can ignore signs. Your participation is appreciated but not required; when we arrived at our first bed-and-breakfast of the trip, the welcome sign read, "Boots, child, and dogs welcome." We obviously walked in one at a time with our children to avoid any unwritten consequences. (True story; grammar matters.)

Other signs of possible peril exist to help keep you alive, so obedience is preferred: "Do not climb" and "Danger! Tree felling in progress," with the image of a giant Christmas tree falling on a person tripping backward. Fortunately, we did not see any trees being felled or anyone being crushed. That didn't mean the danger wasn't real; it just was not a present danger for us in those moments.

Signs come in all shapes and sizes, and red signs, in general, are preventive. The protection a sign offers requires participation: signs are meant to protect, not hinder. Signs tell us what's true, what's required at a certain time and place, and how to prevent unwanted outcomes.

In the same way, we simply cannot extract rules from Scripture without context and apply them to all situations. We also cannot remove love from any of Scripture and have it be the Word of God. God is love. When our rules do not communicate love, care for the person, or compassion, our signs risk miscommunicating our intention, or the purpose of the law in Scripture. Every caution, every law, and most importantly the two laws upon which all others hang (Matthew 22:38–40) were given because God loves us and because we are to love God and each other.

When we read Scripture as a love letter, it lands differently as we invite kids to share their thoughts and feelings about what God is up to throughout the whole of the story. Some things are very clear in the Bible; others require community, prayer, and discernment of the text and its context. In other words, please do not read the pages of Scripture the same way you would a manual for handling hazardous materials. Scripture is nuanced. It is relational. It is historical. It is good. But it is not black-and-white, and we have been warned about legalism.

But it's also true that love corrects. If Scripture is a love letter, I am not discounting that love acts when a person might hurt themselves, take the wrong path, or make a dangerous choice. We can hold up signs. We can love out loud and we can love well. We cannot prevent all bad things or choices with which we disagree. But I also don't think sin should get all the headlines. I could show you the sign of a car half submerged by the incoming tide of the North Sea that read "THIS COULD BE YOU," or I could tell you how to cross safely and that everyone does most days. The sign seems ridiculous if you're already

following the rules—because that sign isn't for you if you'1
following the wisdom of the thousands who have gone befor
you. Some of our kids don't believe that an incoming tide ca1
quickly swamp a car. So put up the sign, and point kids in the
right direction.

When we put up signs, they ought to point toward the
love of Jesus, toward the life he promises us in the fullness of
God—not to all the people who got it wrong. "THIS COULD
BE YOU!" those signs yell as we stay the course. Yet even the
Samaritan woman got a do-over five husbands later. We serve
that same God of do-overs, of try-agains, of *I am with you
always, even to the ends of the earth*, the Lord whose love is
higher, wider, deeper, longer than any ocean's tide. So do you
want to teach your children to swim, or tell them not to try
because they might drown?

Signs, warnings, even the regret of sin can instead point us
back to the gospel. The gospel is *good* news. The story of Jesus
is good. His life is good. He's the headliner. Sin matters—of
course it does. And Jesus was sinless. But starting his story
with what we've done (sin) is like starting this story about a
long walk with a sign that says WARNING! in 156-point font.
It just might not be the best place to start. Signs require our
active participation in observing and heeding their warning.
But they aren't the beginning of the story.

Take time to pause

Signs also teach us what to look for, when to pause, and how
to proceed. If we want kids to know the language of Scripture
(and follow the signs), let's teach it in the context of Scripture. Let's also remember that the language of Scripture can be
weird. Not only is it an ancient text, it has been translated over
and over and deserves to be handled carefully and lovingly. Go

with it. Allow the words that live primarily in the pages red texts (*gospel, salvation, crucifixion, sin, discipleship, ...ption* . . . you know the ones) to be honored by pausing ...nderstanding.

...ry this: When reading or quoting the Bible with kids or ...e less familiar with the vernacular, stop yourself when a ...rd is said that they wouldn't use in everyday life, at the ...ayground, in the grocery store, or while chatting with friends. Ask what it means. Explain what it means. Ask them if they have questions. And carry on. Over time, biblical literacy becomes comprehension, and comprehension becomes action—this is discipleship.

Comprehension is amplified by consistency. Where do we see or hear or feel the same things over and over in the Bible that can teach us how to walk? Years ago I grew curious about where "eyes to see" and "ears to hear" first show up in Scripture. They are common phrases throughout the Bible and are still used today. So who said them first?

My digging found the first iteration of this language shows up in Exodus 3:7–10, and to no surprise, they are the words of God himself in the burning bush, spoken to Moses:

> The LORD said, "I have indeed *seen* the misery of my people in Egypt. I have *heard* them crying out because of their slave drivers, and I am *concerned* about their suffering. So *I have come down to rescue* them from the hand of the Egyptians and to bring them up out of that land into a good and spacious land, a land flowing with milk and honey—the home of the Canaanites, Hittites, Amorites, Perizzites, Hivites and Jebusites. And now *the cry of the Israelites has reached me*, and *I have seen* the way the Egyptians are oppressing them. *So now, go. I am sending you* to Pharaoh to bring my people the Israelites out of Egypt." (italics added for emphasis)

Here's what I see: God not only articulates that what he is seeing and hearing from his children is breaking his heart, but also models that compassion moves him to action and then calls us to follow. The prophets continually call God's people back to "eyes to see" and "ears to hear" so that they would be moved to obedience, repentance, rebuilding, celebration, *so that* God can take up residence among them. And Jesus walks out what this looks like, embodying the very character and nature of God:

- eyes to see the signs,
- ears to hear the warning,
- hearts moved to a compassion that acts,
- *so that we might partner with God to do something about it.*

When we see and hear our kids are struggling with big questions, with pain, with the process of becoming whoever they were made to be, we are invited to allow God to soften our hearts and show compassion. To be moved by our kids in rhythm with God's heart for them. And then to ask Jesus, "What would you have me to do?" Jesus knows the way. And he always has a plan that is for them, for you, and with you.

OPEN SPACES
- Your *presence* matters.
- *Possibilities* are everywhere.

Your presence matters
On that long walk, with her headphones on for most of the day and far enough ahead that she wouldn't have heard me anyway, my kid was largely unaware of my presence. But there were those moments when she realized she was about to crest

a hill or round a bend and I would see her look back. I wasn't walking with her, but more importantly, I imagine, she knew I was there.

We were a day or two into it when my friend came up beside me to check in, chat, and even chase a few of my wonderings. There had been a moment's pause, and he said ever so gently, "She's our leader." I looked up to see that he was looking ahead to my daughter. There she was, well out in front of us, checking the fence post for our waymarker. She glanced back before she climbed the ladder over the fence, and then she proceeded.

I hadn't really noticed (because I was still fairly busy feeling sorry for myself that she didn't want to be with her very cool mother), but I realized then I hadn't ever had to check a waymarker. I don't think I ever wondered which way was the right way. I am absolutely sure that I never once pulled out my map. My head wasn't in the clouds, either; I was simply following my child and never thought to question her way, because she had not given me reason to. Not once.

It never occurred to her to take off in any direction other than the path we were on. It was not her intent to lead us astray. And it was not put upon her to lead; she is simply a leader. And I would not have noticed if I had been beside her or, dare I say, arrogant enough to presume my position was to be out in front of her. If I'm honest, I would have been more likely to question her or double-check the map because why would she know the way? But why would I know the way either? We were navigating new terrain together. She can read. She is smart. She is capable. She didn't *not* need me. She just didn't need me to lead.

There are seasons when we lead, whether out of necessity, stage of life, or intervention when one of our beloveds is off course. But this pilgrimage was not during any of those seasons. I had become the childlike follower.

This is the invitation of Jesus: Follow me. I know the way. Trust me. I will not leave you alone. And the vulnerability of realizing that I had submitted, if even unwittingly, to my child's lead, was a lesson worth repeated reflection. While at first glance the role reversal of it all is quite disarming, it isn't surprising that Jesus had flipped the script. Isn't that his way in his upside-down kingdom? "Let them come . . ."; "The kingdom belongs to such as these . . ."; "Unless you change and become like little children . . ." (Matthew 19:14; Mark 10:14; Luke 18:16; Matthew 18:3). And there I was, following my child up and down the Scottish borders, over fences, past signs and waymarkers that I didn't bother to notice, into wide-open spaces.

Be a guide and a guest. Being a guide and a guest doesn't necessarily mean leading. It means being available, willing, and trusted.

Possibilities are everywhere

The possibility of a big world is scary only if you can't ask questions along the way. Kids must be firmly rooted in who they are and whose they are to navigate this life, regardless of this cultural moment. And they may need you differently than you anticipate. They may also need you to let them be different from what you anticipate. That you are available is sometimes more important than what your experience has to offer.

Wide-open spaces can be terribly uncomfortable for us grownups, though. A fence where we can see all the boundaries is comforting. A gate that swings only one way lets us feel safe. And a gatekeeper of our choosing allows us to police who has access to those inside the fence.

Off in the distance we could see a stone wall, circular, with a small opening on one side. We learned that this would have been used for the sheep at night in the centuries before long fences and land divisions. The shepherd would herd his sheep into the enclosure and then sleep across the opening. It's a lovely image. But it's also what the shepherd does only while the sheep sleep. It's not how they live or grow or feed.

While playpens and cribs serve a very important purpose in the early years, there are many developmental reasons for transitioning our children into open spaces. We hem them in again at night, but we know the value of all the places they visit and explore each day. And the cost of hemming them in at the wrong time of day, so to speak, is high. Keeping our kids safe is not our only job; leading our kids throughout the day so that they can one day lead themselves without us cannot be discounted. It is our privilege to equip them for exploration outside the pen.

Our identity is rooted in the same way our faith is: being confident of what we hope for in Jesus (Hebrews 11:1). Who we were made to be is found in the pages of Scripture. Knowing the Bible helps us know Jesus. Knowing Jesus leads to becoming like Jesus. But if the goal of knowing Scripture is to simply know Scripture, a child may never find their story in its pages, in the same way that keeping them safe by knowing the rules isn't our only hope for their lives.

I think we are sometimes afraid to ask questions, let alone make space for kids to ask questions, because we ourselves don't have all the answers. Sometimes the kids *do* know the answers, though. They *can* lead. When we flip the script and ask kids "What does that mean?" or "Can you help me understand?," they begin to believe that they not only are invited to the conversation but are an essential part of it. They have language for this conversation that we need to learn. Allow them to correct you when you misuse a term or phrase that may mean something different today than it did when you were their age. When we shift our posture to that of a learner, when we sit down, slow down, and even give leadership away, our relationship will be shaped by discipleship and a mutuality that will model Jesus like almost nothing else you can offer them.

The thing is, though my kid was way out in front, I was right there the whole time. I let her let me catch up. No matter how much I wanted to, I didn't yell "Wait for me!" I let her go on ahead. And when I had questions, it was hers to decide whether to engage. Sometimes, I just got to listen to her ask other people questions. Sometimes I listened in as they grew curious about her. I learned a lot about the value of presence and the possibility that it doesn't have to be mine.

We need each other. We were made for community. Whom do your kids need in their community when they'd appreciate having someone other than you to share with or are nervous about the questions they want to ask? Our kids don't necessarily want to tell us when they're struggling with their faith. At least I've found this to be true—maybe it's just me as a parent; maybe it's because I am a pastor. Maybe both. But in any case, our kids need more than their parents: they need real people with real stories and real experiences—even messy ones, even in the middle of a struggle.

Here's why: I think we tend to sanitize Bible stories and turn the people of Scripture into characters in their real-life stories. But they are *real* people. People like you and me. People who have big dreams, who are curious, and who believe with their whole hearts. People who make mistakes. Their relatability is a child's invitation to participation. God can use all people, any people, available people. And God only has

sinners to choose from: people who need do-overs, forgive-
ness, grace, mercy. People like you and me. People who got it
wrong, and people who said yes even when they didn't know
what came next.

If the way we share the Bible doesn't include the reality
of its stories—the human nature of all its characters and the
lavish love of God woven throughout every page, how do kids
make a connection between *that* God and *our* God? We risk
introducing them to a scary God rather than teaching them the
fear of God: reverent awe and wonder for the God of every
possibility, for whom nothing is impossible, the miraculous
Imaginator of all things. If they can't ask questions about the
diversity in the people of Scripture and how their stories inter-
sect with the story of God, our kids may never know God to
be the one who holds all things together with this glorious
thread of love. Worse, they may not be able to receive that
love if they can't relate, or if the stories we tell of who God is
definitively exclude them from the kingdom because of who
they are.

I heard a teen ask an older woman from a local church,
"Do you think I'm going to hell?" That lovely, well-intentioned
woman kept pointing back to Bible verses about sexual immo-
rality and danced around the question, but the teen pressed
her until she said, "I guess I do." How you would answer that
question is none of my business, but I have questions: Why
did that teen ask that question? What have they been told
about Scripture and about their self that led to that in-or-out
moment? And what chance does that child have of ever knowing they are loved and known, invited and included, created by
God for a purpose, if they have been told they're going to hell
anyway? Where do we go from here? The kingdom does not
expand on a fear-based foundation. It just doesn't.

You get to believe what you do about eternity. What I'm asking you to do is believe what Jesus says about all people, especially children. If we are honest with kids about who they are and how loved they are, we get to invite them to be a person of Scripture, too. But that invitation isn't about not going to hell or definitely going to heaven. The invitation is about living on earth as it is in heaven. The kingdom of God is near. It's just one step of many in the same direction that Jesus is traveling.

So much hope and anticipation is woven into the pages of the Bible for those who would come after the final epistles. That's us. All are welcome to participate. All are welcome to find their breath and being in and through and by the Spirit. Our goal in shepherding our kids through conversations about identity is to help them know and believe this. To help them understand the endless invitation to grab ahold of that thread of love, that *tikvah* (the Hebrew word for both hope and rope, defined as the tension a cord can hold when stretched to the full). You don't have to lead them to it. You do not have to be afraid. You can wander in wide-open spaces with one hand on this lifeline and another outstretched in worship. It is enough to be a living vessel, an embodied life of obedience, a testimony that says, "I will serve no other."

What if that is enough? What if your testimony, your story, your identity as a Jesus follower is enough? Obedience is spectacularly curious and flies in the face of social norms. It is a remarkable bright light that cannot be ignored. And it is the only thing you need as you set out into open spaces. Your obedience, your yeses, your nos, your even ifs and even whens are enough of a beacon for those with whom you travel.

17

WHAT IF IT ISN'T SWEET?
(OH, BUT WHAT IF IT IS?)

A few years ago I grew curious about where, how, and when the word *if* shows up in Scripture. It doesn't sound like a word that marks certainty—in fact, it often implies doubt or indecision. But there were three stories where *if* taught me that even in my doubt and indecision, obedience is a steadfast stake in the ground. The word itself is often found in the last phrase spoken by a person about to take a step of obedience. *If* is the linchpin between uncertain and unafraid, and the axle is prayer. And what often hangs in the balance is one's identity.

ESTHER

In chapter 4 of Queen Esther's story, we learn that she has no good choice, and she doubts the plausibility of approaching the king (her husband) because of a law that leads to certain death should she approach him uninvited. Yet if she does not, it means certain death for all Jewish people in the land, including her. Haman, the king's advisor, had convinced him to kill all the Jews in his empire. As Esther weighs whether and how to intervene, she says, "If I perish, I perish" (Esther 4:16), but not before she gives instruction for all Jews to fast and pray for three days.

According to the Hebrew Bible, Esther was born with the name Hadassah. Upon becoming queen of Persia, she used the Persian name Esther to hide her identity. Tellingly, the three-letter root of Esther in Hebrew is *s-t-r*, meaning to hide or conceal. As we read in the text, "Esther did not reveal her people or kindred, for Mordecai had charged her not to tell" (Esther 2:10 NRSVue).

Queen Esther's identity gave her permission (though not protection) to approach the king. Her identity also presumed certain death if Haman's plan was exacted against the Jewish people. Her *if* invited God to do what only God could do in light of who he had called her to be at such a time, and to do what only she could do as the queen.

DANIEL AND FRIENDS

In this story, the four faithful Hebrew captives in Babylon were given new names that represented not only Babylonian culture but also identity. The idea was that if they were renamed and trained to be Babylonian under the customs of King Nebuchadnezzar, their identities would also change to match their names and prescribed behavior: "The king assigned them a daily portion of the royal rations of food and wine. They were to be educated for three years, so that at the end of that time they could be stationed in the king's court" (Daniel 1:5 NRSVue).

Just as it took careful and deliberate commitment for Esther to maintain her identity, though concealed, Daniel, Hananiah, Mishael, and Azariah were intent on remaining faithful to God regardless of their circumstances or the rigorous and forced assimilation.

It was discovered that Shadrach, Meshach, and Abednego (the non-Hebrew names of Daniel's friends) continued to serve the one true God, which outraged King Nebuchadnezzar. Even when threatened to be thrown into a furnace of fire and questioned which god could deliver them from such a threat, they replied:

> O Nebuchadnezzar, we have no need to present a defense to you in this matter. If our God whom we serve is able to deliver us from the furnace of blazing fire and out of your hand, O king, let him deliver us. But *if* not, be it known to you, O king, that we will not serve your gods and we will not worship the golden statue that you have set up. (Daniel 3:16–18 NRSVue, italics added for emphasis)

Their identity defined these men's commitment to both who God says he is and who God said they were. And, spoiler alert: God spared them without even the scent of fire on their cloaks (Daniel 3:27).

JESUS

Jesus' identity also proved to be the reason his life was endangered. Throughout the Gospels, Jesus makes numerous "I am" statements. In the gospel of John, he uses the phrase "I am" seven times to define who he is. And he also uses descriptors that extend "I am," as his Father had. *I am the light of the world. I am the bread of life. I am the living water. I am the good shepherd* . . . At one point, not long before his death, Jesus not only makes one such "I am" statement but also asks Peter who people say he is. "I am the Son of Man," says Jesus. "Who do the people say I am?"

> [His followers] answered, "Some people say you are John the Baptist. Others say you are Elijah. And others say that you are Jeremiah or one of the prophets."

Then Jesus asked them, "And who do you say I am?"

Simon Peter answered, "You are the Christ, the Son of the living God."

Jesus answered, "You are blessed, Simon son of Jonah. No person taught you that. My Father in heaven showed you who I am. So I tell you, you are Peter. And I will build my church on this rock." (Matthew 16:13–17 ICB)

In return for Peter's response, Jesus offers Peter his identity, and the promise he has for him as *Peter*.

If you ever wondered whether Jesus understands what it's like to be persecuted for one's identity, let's just pause here for a moment and acknowledge that, no matter how clear Jesus was about it ("I and the Father are One;" John 10:30), people mistook him for simply a prophet, Elijah, Jeremiah, and even John the Baptist, Jesus' beloved cousin. Bewilderingly, they believed he could be a man who had lived hundreds of years ago, but they could not imagine that he was the Messiah—even though it had been spoken over him and his Father had spoken from heaven that Jesus was his Son, in whom the Father was well pleased (Matthew 3:17).

Jesus was crucified because of his identity. He was not hidden, he did not change his name, he was not ambiguous about his person or his purpose. He was mocked repeatedly, and the fate of his trial rested on who he said (or didn't say) he was. Jesus, our great rabbi in all things, never forgets who he is: as is also true for us, he is who his Father says he is. And God declared him to be his Son.

It is Jesus' *if* moment that compels me to obedience in a moment-to-moment way. Being fully God, yet fully human, he approaches his Father in the garden on the night before his death and asks for favor. Even knowing that he is the embodiment and fulfillment of God's promised deliverance and salvation, he asks: "Father, *if* you are willing, take this cup from me; yet not my will, but yours be done" (Luke 22:42, italics added for emphasis).

In the following hours of his story, we see Jesus' identity lead to his death: "The Jewish leaders insisted, 'We have a law, and according to that law he must die, because he claimed to be the Son of God.'" (John 19:7).

> "Here is your king," Pilate said to the Jews.
>
> But they shouted, "Take him away! Take him away! Crucify him!"
>
> "Shall I crucify your king?" Pilate asked.
>
> "We have no king but Caesar," the chief priests answered. . . .
>
> Pilate had a notice prepared and fastened to the cross. It read: JESUS OF NAZARETH, THE KING OF THE JEWS. . . . The chief priests of the Jews said to Pilate, "Do not write, 'The King of the Jews,' but that this man claimed to be king of the Jews." Pilate answered, "What I have written, I have written." (John 19:14–15, 19, 20–22)

WHO DO YOU SAY YOU ARE?

These three stories urge me to ask one simple but dangerous question: How willing are we as Christians to change our identities until our life matches the meaning of our name, *Christ follower*? "Imitate God, therefore, in everything you do, because you are his dear children. Live a life filled with love, following the example of Christ. He loved us and offered himself as a sacrifice for us, a pleasing aroma to God" (Ephesians 5:1–2 NLT).

Maybe we've just had our priorities skewed. There is an "if" consequence to our kids' identities not being found in Jesus, and I'm not sure we are sufficiently concerned about their knowing what it means to be a Jesus follower. Their identity is made up of so many spectacularly brilliant shiny things that do not catch the light without Jesus. And while we are busy trying to make sure the *right* things are included (like the way we think they should be, or at least not like *that*), it's easy to forget that none of it matters if they do not enter the kingdom of heaven. The parts of who they say they are that we pray will change or be shaped by the Holy Spirit over time can experience that transformation only *with* Jesus. Our priority has to be relationship with Jesus first. And then we get to allow the Holy Spirit to set the priorities thereafter (even if they don't align with ours).

Regardless of where a child finds themselves on their journey of self-discovery and self-expression, we have the divine privilege of introducing them to their identity as one made in God's own image, known and loved, called by Jesus to follow, to belong, and to become more and more like him as a pathway to discover their most authentic self. They can't possibly sort out all the details of how they show up to the conversation before you begin to have it. Can we invite them as they are? Can we look past what we don't understand long enough to see them as Jesus does, and invite him into the possibility of what comes next?

Above all else, what today's kids (and, well, people in general) need to know is that you will sit with them. You will make, and hold, space for them. You will show up for them. You will fix your face when they ask or say something that surprises you, for them. You will stay for as long as it takes, for them.

When there was something important to say or it was important to listen, Jesus sat down. When in doubt, sit down. Ponder longer. Whatever someone is navigating, choosing to stay present will matter more than what you say. What did Jesus do when someone needed him, when they were confused, curious, or uncertain? He went to them, and he sat down. He went for tea with Zacchaeus (Luke 19). He stood between the woman and those who wanted to stone her (John 8). He enjoyed long meals and even longer conversations around the dining table (John 13–16). He fed thousands, but his first instruction after "Feed them" was "Tell everyone to sit down" (Matthew 14:16–19).

We don't have to resolve this tension for today's kids, or even for the church. We need to sit in it, stay present in it, believe for more of Jesus in it, knowing that he alone resolves the tension.

He is the way, the truth, and the life (John 14:6). And the longer I sit in the truth of who he is, the closer I get to the truth about who I am: led by his living and holy Spirit, called to be me fully in his ways, and to have, by his life, my very breath and being. When did that stop being enough for every moment? Do I know what to say to every child lost in their own identity crisis? No. Do I have more questions than answers? Definitely.

But Jesus' ways are simple even when the conversation isn't: ask questions, tell stories, turn to Scripture. Your certainty in who Jesus is does not have to present itself as certainty in every answer. Trusting him is enough. Trust your kids to Jesus. Lead them to him. Let him sit with both of you in hope, and tension, and walk with them as a guide and a guest. What an honor and privilege to do so.

18

WHAT IF WE GET IT WRONG (AND LOSE OUR WAY)?

There came a moment, after climbing one very tall hill, that the possibility of climbing a second very tall hill presented itself. Not because the second hill was on St. Cuthbert's Way, but rather because it was in front of us and the kids asked, "Are we climbing that one, too?" (But not the way I was asking it, with quivering legs. They asked it the way kids do: like climbing hills is fun.) My instinct was to check the map, check with our facilitator, check the waymarkers, all certain to lead us along the *right* path. The instinct of my friend, the other, more fun mum, was to ask, "Do you want to?"

A bit stunned, I felt myself holding back every desire to tackle her, jump in, and ask a better question, in my opinion: something along the lines of "Is it part of the pilgrimage?" or "Is it even the right direction?" "*Is that necessary?*" Having conquered a hill called Holyrood, and knowing the name of the next hill to be Morebattle, what would you choose at twelve years old? Does it not sound majestic to conquer Morebattle? The adults fell at the mercy of the two kids (if not with a glint of side-eye toward Danielle, the better mother) and we followed their lead up the second hill.

Now, a hill isn't simply a hill. There are certain ways up and only certain ways down, and a hill being round, so to speak, with a 360-degree view from the top, it can feel quite disorienting after ensuring you've captured a panoramic photo of the moment. Which way did we come up? Which way are we headed? Which direction is our next meal? And between the lack of a signal for Google Maps and uncertainty as to which direction was up on our printed map, once again, we asked the kids to choose.

As wild and ridiculous as this all sounds, there are a few things to keep in mind:

1. The kids were not alone. We were not agreeing to certain death.
2. The consequences of their choices would be shared and carried by their grownups.
3. The worst-case-scenario was that our friend Ang would come and pick us up in the Sunshine Van and take us all for fish and chips. (It was called the Sunshine Van because she was in it.)

The stakes were low, but our (adult) legs were tired, and the sun was dipping into the horizon. What we did know for sure was that the way forward was down.

As the light faded and dusk set in, we listened for traffic. Surely, cars are a sign of life (and a path to where we were going from wherever we were)! We could see a road on the other side of the woods, and until this moment, the best way toward our destination had been *through*. Into the woods we went, when suddenly Ian, our often-more-subtle-than-I-would-prefer facilitator, exclaimed, "Watch your step!" Danielle was about to set her foot down in a barbed wire trap full of dead fish. We soon realized the entire forest floor was laced with barbed wire (and we were not the prey of choice).

All we had to do was get to the other side (that joke about the chicken doesn't land quite the same way anymore). Move toward the sound of the road. Move toward the other fence line. In the absence of a waymarker (we had certainly lost Cuthbert by this point), surely there would be an opening, a gate, or a ladder. There was not. Using a stump, a tree branch, and a fence post, we hoisted ourselves over the fence, whose top rung was more loosely strung barbed wire.

Not surprisingly, when we figured out where we were, it was evident that we had lost significant ground and had over five miles still to go. There were no sidewalks, and everyone except me thought we had walked far enough for one day. If it had been up to me, I would have stuck to the path, retraced our steps, found the waymarker, and fixed the problem. Five miles felt fair after choosing to deviate from the path. This wouldn't have happened if we hadn't asked the kids, I thought. And just as quickly as that thought entered, I realized that this has got to be the issue at least half the time: that we *don't* ask the children, not that we *do*.

The stories we have of that single hour of our day could fill another book altogether. We didn't just let them lead; they chose to lead. They could have said, "Don't make me decide." They could have defaulted to dependence. But they didn't. There were wide-open spaces to explore, and they were up to the challenge. And we all would have missed out on sweet Ang pulling up in the Sunshine Van, tunes blaring, face smiling, horn beeping, hand waving to greet us as she came to our rescue, delightfully unaware of our death-defying ordeal (clearly, I'm still recovering).

Danielle turned to the kids and said, "Remember this: You can always phone a friend. No matter where you are, no matter what you have done, always know who you can call."

I want to be that person. I want to be the one who kids know they can call. I want to be the first one they think of when they don't know what to do because I want the opportunity to love them, sit with them, show up for them, and just be present with them. This is the way of Jesus. Be the one who shows up, no matter what it is you're showing up to. You are the adult. You know how to find the way home. *This* is your chance to lead. Lead them to Jesus.

There is always a way back to the path. There is always a way home. There is always an invitation. This is what love is like—God is love, and Jesus is what God is like. As you imagine what the invitation would look like—perhaps it's a fun and whimsical one with glitter and rainbows, perhaps it is formal and costly, maybe it's a text or a verbal "You should definitely come!"—work hard not to fill out the line that says "When" unless you can put "Always" where a time or date would normally appear.

Galatians 6:9–10 encourages us, "So let us not grow weary in doing what is right, for we will reap at harvest time, if we do not give up. So then, whenever we have an opportunity, let us work for the good of all and especially for those of the family of faith" (NRSVue). There is always a way back for you, too. You have not failed. You are not alone. God is for you and with you. God's love is for you. As you receive your invitation, it will not fail to share abundant evidence with the kids in your life that our God can be trusted, he is good, and he is love.

19

EVERY BIBLE STORY *IS* AN IDENTITY STORY

When it comes to asking questions about our identity, I think we have all been there. Some of us have been there a few times. Others return to the same question over and over again throughout life: "Who am I?" While the conversation has also come to include larger questions about the nature and definition of identity, we will likely agree that who I am, and who you are, is at the heart of it. Our experience of the word has shape-shifted in real time, and if we are not careful, it may appear that one's identity is simply a sum of parts, or the loudest part, or the most painful part, or the most private part, even the most public part, the best part, or the parts we choose to share and even the parts we work to hide.

If I listen to the world's definition, my identity is who I say I am, and you get to simply accept it. But this is a one-dimensional definition. I am certain that who I say I am is part of my identity, but how you see me (whether right or wrong), whom I identify with, the things I like, how I spend my time, what I believe, what you *think* I believe, and what you see on social media or in real life also contribute to how my identity is revealed. You may not get to decide what my identity is, but you can piece together a pretty accurate picture of who I am by being part of my life if I'm honest, genuine, and authentic.

Here enters the authenticity paradox.

The Word of God, as both the Bible and Jesus himself, spends every story unpacking identity differently. But there is a common theme. The identity of every person or people group in Scripture is defined one way: who God says they are. People wrongly identify others countless times in the Bible, but most often those are cases of false identity, misconception, or concealed identity.

As I run through the "hall of heroes" in Hebrews 11, picking favorites to make my point, I see that every single testimony of each person named is a story of identity. The list isn't exhaustive, so add your favorites to it and ask yourself: Is there even one story in the whole of Scripture that does not hinge on a person's identity, whether they betray it, rise to it, or stand firm in it? Kings and kingdoms rose and fell at God's command, most often because Israel forgot who they were or fell victim to an ungodly leader who had chosen the power of his appointment over the privilege of his anointing.

The whole of Scripture is a story of identity—finding it and losing it, choosing it and being robbed of it, submitting to it and undervaluing it, chasing it and forgetting it. But the story of the gospel is one of setting identity once for all time, and the story of the cross is that of Jesus being murdered for claiming to be who he is.

Abram becomes Abraham.

Sarai becomes Sarah.

Jacob becomes Israel.

Esau becomes second.

Joseph becomes regal.

Moses becomes Egyptian, only to return to his people and be Hebrew, from prince to shepherd to leader.

David, a shepherd boy, is found and anointed, runs into hiding, and is then appointed king yet loses his way.

Hadassah becomes Esther.

Gideon becomes brave.

Elijah reveals God's identity.

Ahaz rejects his identity while his son, Hezekiah, redeems his, only for his son, Manasseh, to betray the family name once again.

Daniel and friends stand firm.

Mary finds favor because of who she is.

Joseph believes in Mary's calling.

The disciples drop everything that defines them for the One who calls them.

Jesus is God's Son.

Is it any wonder that identity is the capstone of faith, of self-actualization, of surrender, of hope, when Jesus himself was born to be someone other than the world was expecting? I guess what I'm trying to say is that this conversation about identity is not optional: how we know who we are depends on Whose we are. The leap of faith to be called child of God not only changes every other definition we have put on or had put on us—every single label, every facet of the prism in the kaleidoscope pales in comparison and is ordered in light of this truth. I am a child of God first. All else submits to this promise. And if anything I say about who I am betrays this truth, it has to go. But there is so much to who I am that is also brilliant because of this truth, and it is not disqualified as I align with what it means to be an image bearer.

Knowing who I am, and choosing to measure it all against my sense of belonging in the kingdom, is the lid of the jigsaw puzzle box. If the piece doesn't fit, I get to let it go. I do not have to push, bend, or carry any piece of me that does not agree with how God sees me. This has to matter most. And where it matters as the adult invited close on a child's walk of faith is that a child's identity in Jesus must matter more than any of the other claims on their identity that they or others are making about them. We get to prioritize their kingdom status over all else and invite them to do the same.

CHOOSING TO REMEMBER CHILDHOOD

While I sit in a treehouse like a little girl living her childhood dreams of world travel and play and big ideas brought to life, I remember five-year-old me kneeling by her bed asking God why I was made a girl if I wasn't useful in the church. Why would God make me the way I am, full of wonder and questions, always talking, always imagining, if I wasn't welcome to be fully me in his house? Wouldn't it just have been easier if God had made me a boy?

To be clear, these were not the sorrowful questions of a transgender child (although they could be); this was the heart's cry of an oppressed girl being told who she was instead of being asked who she was made to be.

I have sat with that memory many times as I contemplated where to begin with this conversation. We need to contend with more than a few issues as the church, especially as parents and leaders raising kids and having different conversations from when we were children. It has been difficult for the church, and for parents, to keep up. As we reconcile the gaps created by not having this conversation, we must also recognize and reconcile the scars left by patriarchy and the ways that too many people have been hurt by the church—either by the conversations or by the unwillingness to have them—and grieve the many who knew they were no longer welcome. I was no longer welcome. You may need to name and process some wounds or scars. You may need to repent of having caused some, unknowingly or otherwise. But know that most of us still have so many questions, and that's okay as long as we create safe space to ask them.

- What does equity even mean? Do we under-stand mutuality?
- The church has not stewarded the beauty and blessing of two genders well, so why are we surprised that it is struggling to understand, let alone welcome, every-one else?
- Where do we continue to prop up patriarchy, including the idolatry of the feminine and masculine constructs that keep our kids from fully showing up, fully partici-pating, fully feeling safe?

We have inadvertently *and* intentionally, even sometimes by our own strength, upheld social dynamics that have crippled, broken, and rejected generations of marginalized peoples. But patriarchy has rarely walked past a society or culture with-out preying on the hubris of those who stand to gain power, wealth, control. And while this book does not dive into the deep depravity and damage of patriarchy that continues to abuse our young, sully our mirrors with body dysmorphia, and weaponize itself against anyone who isn't a cisgender, het-erosexual, white male, I would be remiss (and foolish) not to name it.

Since its institutionalization, the church has been unwel-coming at best to the gifts, talents, abilities, and leadership of most others, and this issue remains at the center of many debates. But God's image is within every single human being (yes, everyone), and that is spectacular. And we are missing out on the fully magnificent reflection of this image by deciding *on behalf of God* who is welcome to express that image, God's own imagination, God's creativity on display. This is not okay. This is not the heart of God, and it is not the way of Jesus.

So let's proceed slowly, with caution, through a conversation that very few truly want to have. Most of us know we need to have it, and some are desperate to have had it yesterday; but you might want questions answered, clarity for your already formed theology, specific rights and wrongs plainly laid out. Let's not do that to one another anymore. Allow God's abundant grace to lead you—you have been loved in your unloveliest moments. You have been accepted by your Creator—he thinks you're delightful, by the way—made to be a living stone to build a house of worship (1 Peter 2) and abundantly able to be filled with the Spirit of the light of the world. Let's start there. And if there is confusion or disagreement along the journey, could you express it in the form of a question? I believe this is the gentlest way forward, and I am committed to the gentleness of gracious questions.

I was fifteen years old, fully invested in my church, attending (and running) all kinds of programs four days a week, when the senior pastor and three deacons showed up at the front door of our family home. They had come to "rebuke me in the name of Jesus Christ" (their watermarked, wax-sealed, signed-with-a-calligraphy-pen letter confirmed this) and asked for a public flogging, so to speak (confession and repentance in front of the church "family," the sort of trauma you read about in religious thrillers and cult accounts). What was my crime? I spoke up. I combed the Scriptures for how to bring forward a situation that did not at all look like what I thought Jesus would want, and I used my voice. For this, I was rebuked. Well, that, and the gall of questioning a pastor as a fifteen-year-old child.

The only part of this story I want you to remember is that I was a child. For most kids, that would have been the end of God, belief, faith, hope, church. For me, I went deeper into the New Testament and camped out in 1 John 3 and 4, memorizing the definition of love. After three months of reading and rereading this text, I found my identity embedded in the Word of God:

Child of God.

Beloved.

I am to be *like him*:

Pure just as he is pure,

righteous,

loving,

life laid down for others.

Little children, let us love not in word or speech but in deed and truth. And by this we will know that we are from the truth and will reassure our hearts before him whenever our hearts condemn us, for God is greater than our hearts, and he knows everything. Beloved, if our hearts do not condemn us, we have boldness before God, and we receive from him whatever we ask, because we obey his commandments and do what pleases him. (1 John 3:18–22 NRSVue)

Now don't miss this next part, because the commandment is laid out for us:

And this is his commandment, that we should believe in the name of his Son Jesus Christ and love one another, just as he has commanded us. All who obey his commandments abide in him, and he abides in them. And by this we know

that he abides in us, by the Spirit that he has given us.
(vv. 23–24 NRSVue)

Obeying leads to abiding. Obeyers are abiders, and this
is made known by God's own Spirit abiding in us. Imagine.
Imagine this unimaginable truth: the Spirit of the living God
indwells us when we believe in Jesus and love one another.
And as difficult as either one of those can be in a season, a conversation, a moment, or a decision, it is not too much to ask.
God has only ever asked of us what he also made us capable
of: God fit us with his own image made to bring him glory, so
surely he fit us with enough capacity to love one another. If
God is love, and I am made to reflect him to those around me,
I already have all the love I will need to obey his commandments so that God's Spirit may abide in me. What a wonder!
What a gift. What a joy!

Some of us want to focus on all the other commandments,
but I believe that if we get these two right, love God and love
one another, we may very well get to stop talking about the
rest. But I feel quite certain that we have not yet collectively
committed to love the way Scripture commands. We have
terms and conditions. We have built guardrails and fences,
made rules and lists that only the inner circle decides and reg-
ulates, but we all know what they are. We all know whether
we are welcome or not. We all know who's included because
we know how country clubs work, no matter whether we've
ever been invited inside one.

Even if we decided to hold fast to the Levitical law on
top of every do or don't of Paul's letters and chose to look
past context, era, circumstance at the time of these writings, I
would still argue, in agreement with Jesus, that they all build
on the only commandments he himself ever gave: "'You shall

love the Lord your God with all your heart, and with all your soul, and with all your mind.' This is the greatest and first commandment. And a second is like it: 'You shall love your neighbor as yourself.' On these two commandments hang all the Law and the Prophets" (Matthew 22:37–40 NRSVue).

In 2020, I listened through the Bible while walking (think pandemic cabin fever), and I was prepared for Leviticus to be a slog. So much splattering of blood, so many scapegoats, so many rules. I asked the Lord to whisper in my ear while I listened because this was a lot, and I'm a visual person, so there was quite a picture being painted in my imagination.

I welled up with tears one day as I realized the exchange that was at play in Leviticus: this list was what was required for the Lord of Armies, God himself, to take up residence among his children. *If you can make a place of welcome, on earth as it is in heaven, I will come. I have come before, and I will do it again and again.* And I heard a still, small voice say, "I've always believed in my kids. I made them capable of all this and more. It was never too much to ask for holiness to come and abide. If they could do that for me, I would come and be with them. And they would be made holy. But I gave them a choice, and I've given you one, too."

I cannot help but believe Jesus' words. What if we actually love the Lord that much, and loved all that he created (our neighbors and ourselves included) enough to take the love we have for God and allow ourselves to be filled with abiding until it overflows such that others might know this great love? Isn't there enough for everyone? Or is it that you'd prefer your neighbor not be included? Or perhaps it's difficult to love them because you have not received God's love for yourself, so loving others like you love yourself is messy and complicated and doesn't look much like love in the end.

Beloved, you are worthy of God's love. You are worthy of belief. You are welcome to obey and abide just as you are today. His is a kingdom of lavish overflow where there is always more than enough. Always. You aren't late, and it's not too late. You have the image of the Creator knit into your being, and I am just so curious about it. What do I get to know about God because you chose to show up clothed in his glory? Who told you that who you thought you could be as a child wasn't for you? Where did it all fall apart? When did you stop believing?

This is a complex conversation, and it requires the pursuit of the presence of God, joy in your own obedience and abidance, and a love that knows no boundaries. We are to love one another. And the King of kings believes both that it is possible and that God made us capable. He also knows it's not too much to ask in exchange for the presence of holiness, the very Spirit of the living God.

Beloved, let us love one another, because love is from God; everyone who loves is born of God and knows God. Whoever does not love does not know God, for God is love. God's love was revealed among us in this way: God sent his only Son into the world so that we might live through him. In this is love, not that we loved God but that he loved us and sent his Son to be the atoning sacrifice for our sins. Beloved, since God loved us so much, we also ought to love one another. No one has ever seen God; if we love one another, God abides in us, and his love is perfected in us.

By this we know that we abide in him and he in us, because he has given us of his Spirit. And we have seen and do testify that the Father has sent his Son as the Savior of the world. God abides in those who confess that Jesus is the

Son of God, and they abide in God. So we have known and believe the love that God has for us.

God is love, and those who abide in love abide in God, and God abides in them. Love has been perfected among us in this: that we may have boldness on the day of judgment, because as he is, so are we in this world. There is no fear in love, but perfect love casts out fear; for fear has to do with punishment, and whoever fears has not reached perfection in love. We love because he first loved us. Those who say, "I love God," and hate a brother or sister are liars, for those who do not love a brother or sister, whom they have seen, cannot love God, whom they have not seen. The commandment we have from him is this: those who love God must love their brothers and sisters also.

Everyone who believes that Jesus is the Christ has been born of God, and everyone who loves the parent loves the child. By this we know that we love the children of God, when we love God and obey his commandments. For the love of God is this, that we obey his commandments. And his commandments are not burdensome, for whatever is born of God conquers the world. And this is the victory that conquers the world, our faith. Who is it who conquers the world but the one who believes that Jesus is the Son of God? (1 John 4:7–5:5 NRSVue)

Love is not designed to be burdensome. It is the great overcomer of fear, and our faith—through belief, obedience, and abiding—is enough to conquer the world. Go well, conquerors. Be brave. Have a conversation that looks like Love. And remember that love always looks like an invitation.

There is power in the art of invitation. Come and sit. Come and be. Come with your curiosity and imagination open to the possibility of whom you might find and what you might learn. But however you do, please just come. That's the invitation of love. There is a warm welcome and a radical hospitality to the invitation itself; but to discover all that the invitation entails is a wonder all its own.

This is my experience of God's love. It is the kind of gorgeous invitation you leave on your fridge long after the event has come and gone simply to remind you of its beauty. You are invited. All are welcome. You are loved. Come, play, wander, breathe, be. Because this invitation doesn't have a date that comes or goes. It's always there. It's always today on this invitation.

PSALM 8

LORD, our Lord,
   how majestic is your name in all the earth!

You have set your glory
   in the heavens.
Through the praise of children and infants
   you have established a stronghold against your enemies,
   to silence the foe and the avenger.
When I consider your heavens,
   the work of your fingers,
the moon and the stars,
   which you have set in place,
what is mankind that you are mindful of them,
   human beings that you care for them?

You have made them a little lower than the angels
   and crowned them with glory and honor.
You made them rulers over the works of your hands;
   you put everything under their feet:
all flocks and herds,
   and the animals of the wild,
the birds in the sky,
   and the fish in the sea,
   all that swim the paths of the seas.

LORD, our Lord,
   how majestic is your name in all the earth!

ACKNOWLEDGMENTS

This conversation started a long time ago for me, but it is because of a few remarkable people that I had the courage to keep asking questions, say difficult things in unwelcoming spaces, and wrestle with God as the Spirit asked me to press in, keep going, and dream of more for today's kids.

As I began to speak on the topic of identity, I would often say, "I don't have a pony in this race," meaning this is not an "issue" I felt that I was facing personally in any way. But that's simply not true. Sitting at tables with friends, colleagues, and thought leaders far better equipped to steward this conversation than me, I began to ache for the kids who might never know the love of Jesus because of the invitation not extended to them just as they are. Among those tremendous humans who entertained (and tolerated) my questions, my ignorance, and my learning curve, I owe a debt of gratitude, and in the words of the apostle Paul, "I thank my God every time I remember you. In all my prayers for all of you, I always pray with joy because of your partnership in the gospel from the first day until now, being confident of this, that he who began a good work in you will carry it on to completion until the day of Christ Jesus" (Philippians 1:3–6).

Mum and Dad, thank you for leaving the church with me the day I was kicked out as a kid. Thank you for doubling down on me instead of religion. Thank you for the sacrifice that I know it cost you: the friends who abandoned you, who never called to see whether we were okay, the ones who told their kids to shun me at school. Thank you for keeping your faith not only in me, but in Jesus, who is so much more than what we were shown in that season.

Ruby, Benaiah, Elliotte, and Matthew: You have given a lot to make space for this book. From dinner conversations that got hijacked by my big questions to evenings where I sat glued to my laptop and literally ignored you (sorry about that), thank you for knowing that this work mattered enough to release me to do it. Thank you for letting me be awkward and inappropriate and ignorant as I learned, and thank you for being brave enough to call it all out and offer different words, alternative vantage points, the safety to be wrong and to be corrected. I pray that you always know who you were made to be, and that space was created for you to learn who that is because of the space you afforded me on this journey.

Kim, for the countless hours on FaceTime reading chapters and ideas and questions to you; for the number of tears you shed with me as I doubted myself or this project and the compassion you showed me as you propped me back up and told me to get back to work (because I was made for this); for believing I was made for this; for the pounds of confetti you have thrown in my direction: I will spend the rest of my life saying thank you. You are one of the best gifts that God has ever given me, and I will love you mosterest from here to Everest forever.

Sarah, your ability to make space for people is divine. Those hours on your front porch talking about what our kids are experiencing and how we can come alongside them, support them, and respond schooled me in my biases, my privilege, and my false certainties. Thank you for being gentle with me. Thank you for loving me enough to stay in the conversation. Thank you for introducing me to the possibility of more and better for this generation. Thank you for pushing me, for knowing you could, and for never settling theologically.

My dear Adrienne, thank you for calling out the warrior in me and never letting me off the hook. Your invitation to the enchanted forest changed everything. Thank you for believing in me and what God had deposited into me in a way that I did not yet believe for myself. And thank you for the introduction to the ever-exuberant gracious hosts of said forest, Mattie and Bill Ferg. I do not know what you have done to domesticate even the sparrows in your garden, but I am so grateful for your invitation to call the Pine Cone home and literally craft and cobble these words together in a treehouse with three dogs snuggled at my feet and a butterfly perched on the edge of my laptop. Thank you for your radical hospitality. It was heavenly.

The time I spent working with the team at RaiseUpFaith gave me the courage and tenacity for this conversation. Paul, thank you for prioritizing this work and for praying without ceasing. Christine, you make my whimsy make sense. Thank you for being a rock—the most organized, thoughtful, wise rock. Natalie, I will always be a fangirl. Your dream of a better gospel story for kids, *One Story*, was the beginning of my dream for the same. Jo, thank you for believing that mountains can, indeed, be moved. I know the voice of Jesus better because of how he sounds when you speak truth over me.

Danielle Strickland, Boundless, Infinitum, Ian, Ang, Ellie, and Judah: the Long Walk was the beginning of this book, and you were not only the best companions, but the best teachers. The nuggets of wisdom you dropped along the way were a breadcrumb trail of hope, Danielle. Ian, the way you see people, like really see them, made me feel seen and made me want to have eyes like Jesus in the most profound way. Ang, your joy in all circumstances is a healing balm, and your laughter is what I hope heaven sounds like. Judah, you are a delight of curiosity and knowledge intertwined with a compassionate spirit unlike many kids your age I've met. Ellie, thanks for coming along and allowing me to just be with you. You are a marvel and a tremendous leader.

Dr. Mark Baker, the work you did with *Centered-Set Church* sent my speaking and writing on a trajectory for which I have you to thank. I can't say enough about all I've learned from you, including the way my imagination was sparked to challenge kids' pastors and parents to think differently about what they see when they look at their kids and to help them watch for orientation toward Jesus first.

Dr. Mark Yarhouse, I wept for two days as I sat at a table in Florida listening to you unpack not only the psychology of identity and some of what we are seeing and experiencing today, but also a gospel-centric understanding of identity. Your humble posture was Christlike, your gentleness was hope-filled, and your care for people navigating this conversation from myriad perspectives was a masterclass in integrity. Thank you for the work you have done and continue to do. In the words of Preston Sprinkle, you truly are the Master Yoda of this conversation.

Lastly, thank you, Jesus, for entrusting this conversation to me. I pray I have stewarded it the way I believe you asked me to. I remember being asked to write a curriculum centering on identity a few years ago, and I said no at first. The encounter I had with the Holy Spirit as I reimagined that inclusive gospel years prior had given me enough content and enough creativity, I thought, for a lifetime. But the publisher asked me to pray about it. "Jesus, I asked you for words once before, and it was enough for me," I prayed. "I would never ask you twice. But I have been asked to ask if you have more you want to say through me." And Jesus whispered, "I hope you ask me more than twice." Thank you, Jesus, for the way you speak and invite us to ask for more and pray outlandish prayers. I audaciously ask that we do this again sometime. I love you.

NOTES

CHAPTER 4

1. A mind map is a visual tool that helps organize information showing relationships among pieces of the whole. It is often created around a single concept. See, e.g., "What Is a Mind Map?," MindMapping, accessed April 4, 2024, https://www.mindmapping.com/mind-map.

CHAPTER 6

1. The Google Books Ngram Viewer is a tool for charting the use of a word or words in printed texts across time. To track the use of *identity*, enter the word in the search tool at https://books.google.com/ngrams/.

2. This is a common quote found several places. See, e.g., Neil Strauss, *The Truth: An Uncomfortable Book about Relationships* (Edinburgh: Canongate Books, 1992); *Alcoholics Anonymous Big Book*, 4th ed. (New York: Alcoholics Anonymous World Services, 2002).

3. Mark Yarhouse, *Understanding Gender Dysphoria: Navigating Transgender Issues in a Changing Culture* (Lisle: IVP Academic, 2015).

4. *Cisgender* describes a person whose gender identity corresponds with the identity of their sex assigned at birth.

CHAPTER 7

1. Miroslav Volf, *Allah: A Christian Response* (San Francisco: HarperOne, 2011), 165. Italics in the original.

2. Jewish Virtual Library, s.v. "Hospitality," accessed April 20, 2024, https://www.jewishvirtuallibrary.org/hospitality. Quoting Shabbat 127a–b in the Babylonian Talmud.

3. "The Jewish Value of Hospitality," My Jewish Learning, January 31, 2023, https://www.myjewishlearning.com/article/jewish-hospitality/.

CHAPTER 8

1. James D. Fearon, "What Is Identity (as We Now Use the Word)?," Department of Political Science, Stanford University, November 3, 1999, 1–3, https://web.stanford.edu/group/fearon-research/cgi-bin/wordpress/wp-content/uploads/2013/10/What-is-Identity-as-we-now-use-the-word-.pdf.

2. Dictionary.com, s.v. "identity," accessed April 16, 2024, https://www.dictionary.com/browse/identity.

CHAPTER 9

1. Victoria Bennett, "Loneliness on the Rise: Why Our Social Groups are the Perfect Antidote," LinkedIn, March 10, 2023, https://www.linkedin.com/pulse/loneliness-rise-why-our-social-groups-perfect-antidote-bennett/.

2. The ideas in the following paragraphs are drawn from Mark D. Baker, *Centered-Set Church: Discipleship and Community without Judgmentalism* (Downers Grove: IVP Academic, 2021). See especially chapter 2, "Bounded, Fuzzy, and Centered Churches."

CHAPTER 11

1. "Map of Ancient Roman Samaria—Map of Samaria at the Time of Jesus," Conforming to Jesus Ministry, last modified June 29, 2013, https://www.conformingtojesus.com/charts-maps/en/map_of_ancient_roman_samaria.htm.

2. Lawrence H. Schiffman, "The Samaritan Schism," Biblical Archaeology Society, August 11, 2014, https://www.biblicalarchaeology.org/daily/ancient-cultures/daily-life-and-practice/the-samaritan-schism/.

3. "10 Surprising Lessons from the Parable of the Good Samaritan," Becoming Christians, November 17, 2021, https://becomingchristians.com/lessons-from-the-parable-of-the-good-samaritan/.

4. "What Is a Samaritan?," GotQuestions, June 24, 2019, https://www.gotquestions.org/what-is-a-Samaritan.html.

5. BAS staff, "Understanding the Good Samaritan Parable," Biblical Archaeology Society, December 27, 2023, https://www.biblicalarchaeology.org/daily/archaeology-today/archaeologists-biblical-scholars-works/understanding-the-good-samaritan-parable/.

CHAPTER 14

1. Deloitte is a multinational professional services network. Their Gen Z and Millennial survey includes over twenty thousand respondents in over forty countries. Deloitte, *2023 Gen Z and Millennial Survey: Waves of Change: Acknowledging Progress, Confronting Setbacks* (Deloitte Global, 2023), https://www.deloitte.com/content/dam/assets-shared/legacy/docs/deloitte-2023-genz-millennial-survey.pdf.

2. Deloitte, 3.

3. Deloitte, 3.

4. Victoria Rideout and Michael B. Robb, *The Common Sense Census: Media Use by Kids Age Zero to Eight, 2020* (San Franciso: Common Sense Media, 2020), 4, https://www.commonsensemedia.org/sites/default/files/research/report/2020_zero_to_eight_census_final_web.pdf.

5. Deloitte, 2023 *Gen Z and Millennial Survey*, 4.

6. Deloitte, 4.

7. Deloitte, 4.

CHAPTER 15

1. Barna Group and Awana, *Children's Ministry in a New Reality: Building Church Communities That Cultivate Lasting Faith* (Ventura: Barna Group, 2022). As a Christian research organization, Barna provides data and insights about present-day trends in faith, culture, and ministry.

CHAPTER 16

1. Imagers are people who don't just bear the image of God but are the embodied image of God. Not one of us embodies it fully, which requires us to need each other to learn more about the creativity, imagination, character, and nature of God. For further insight, see Preston Sprinkle, "What Does It Mean to Be God's Image? Dr. Carmen Imes," May 22, 2023, in *Theology in the* Raw, podcast, YouTube Video, 54:25, https://www.youtube.com/watch?v=pk0Oh1VUX9o.

THE AUTHOR

Christie Penner Worden is a strategic leader, speaker, preacher, and writer who is passionate about discipling children, inspiring leaders, and equipping churches with effective support to raise this generation with courageous faith. Christie is a pastor with the Be In Christ (BIC) denomination. She has an Engage Certificate in children's ministry through Bethel Seminary and is a certified coach with the International Network of Children's Ministry. She loves sharing her wonder and what-ifs with dreamers and doers alike, and with organizations including Jesus Collective, David C. Cook, Ministry Spark, INCM, New Wine, CTA Kids, KidzMatter, Awesome KidMin Community, Lead Volunteers, Kids Ministry Collective, *Collide Kids Podcast*, *Bible Talk*, and 1230 Kids as well as national denominations and local churches across Canada.